Women Rescuers of WWII

True stories of the unsung women heroes who rescued refugees and Allied servicemen in WWII

Elise Baker

losses, direct or indirect, that are incurred as a result of the use of the information contained within this document, including, but not limited to, errors, omissions, or inaccuracies.

Table of Contents

Introduction

Figure 1. Jewish families in Warsaw, Poland being evicted from their homes.

When there is nowhere safe to go, where do you take your next step? When there is no one you can trust, whom do you rely on? When your whole world collapses around you, what holds you steady?

Most people in the West today have never had to face these questions, but in and around Europe during the Second World War (WWII), people in their millions did, and some brave individuals stepped up to try and answer when the solutions were anything but obvious.

It is easy to forget—sometimes too easy—how human kinship and compassion seem to be dwindling as the 21st century progresses. We are consumed by the events of our fast-paced lives and do not have time to build a reference from the past that could clarify the actions we take today. Studying the past helps us remember what is important and how to engage in the complexity of the present.

Brave women paved the way during WWII, and we can all learn a lot from their courage. It is therefore crucial to shine a light on these incredible women's stories. We won't find them in school textbooks, so let's do the work to honor them and learn from them.

This book is part of my series *Brave Women Who Changed the Course of WWII*. It focuses on the struggles and triumphs of women from around the world, young and old, who stepped out when the world said: "Stay at home and keep quiet."

It is not another book about the horrors and atrocities of WWII, but rather a celebration of the courage and compassion of eight brave women who risked their own lives to save those of the persecuted and the hunted. It is full of important historical facts about WWII that are colored in with inspirational and sometimes comical personal accounts of women standing up against antisemitism and male prejudice during the era. But before we jump too far ahead, we need to understand the origins of WWII and the main players.

The Beginnings of WWII

The true beginnings of WWII date back to the end of the Great War, when the Treaty of Versailles was signed by the victors. France, Great Britain, and the USA laid down the path to peace in the hope that the world would never see another war, but in doing so, they needed Germany to accept the blame. The stipulations were that Germany had to pay reparations to the victors, reduce its military, and most importantly, release the territories it had conquered in Europe.

But after WWI, German leaders and citizens were outraged and hell-bent on regaining their pride and economic freedom once again. Internal conflict ensued that manifested in protests and general economic downfall. Just as Germany started to see some positive economic growth again, the Great Depression took hold and created enormous stress on the country as well as the rest of the world. If fingers were being pointed at Germany for their mistakes, then in turn, Germany would point fingers at someone else for their failures and weaknesses.

Needing to improve their livelihoods and regain political power, Germany made some big changes to their country in the 10 years or so before WWII. Their fascist agenda aimed to remove everything within their borders that were not purely Germanic (both in looks and in traditional ideals) and then do the same in neighboring countries.

To conquer people's ideals and values was the first plan of action. Next, they would unite all citizens under their Aryan race into a larger conquering power. Germany was not going to let the world think less of them. If they were not to be respected and included, then they would *take* their respect by force.

Having said that, the stories we will be looking at do not solely revolve around the six years of WWII (1939–1945), but also during the years prior, when the terror in central Europe was just beginning to show. As far back as 1933, the Jewish population read the news and feared that their homes and livelihoods would be stripped away from them in a fury of fascist ideals. WWII started much earlier for those living in Germany, France, Czechoslovakia, and Poland.

As Hitler began making outlandish statements, people were shaking their heads in disagreement and horror. These were not the outpourings of the typical military rivalry made 25 years earlier in WWI, but far more deadly and persecutory ideas based on racial theories that led to actions that would change the world forever. Dictatorships arose in Spain, Germany, Italy, and Japan, whose tyrannical philosophies started to infiltrate the rest of Europe and then the world. They pressured other countries to either conform or submit to fascist sentiments.

WWII began in earnest in 1939, instigated by Adolf Hitler, the leader of the Axis forces of Germany and its fellow fascist countries, including, for a period, the communist forces of the Soviet Union. Days after

Hitler signed a nonaggression pact with Russia's leader Josef Stalin, Hitler invaded Poland from the west on September 1, 1939. Two days later, Britain and France declared war on Germany. Two weeks later, Russia invaded Poland from the east and the country fell quickly.

Although the terror in Europe had been going on for years in pockets, it was only in 1939 that the news of severe persecution and killings began to break to the rest of the world through radio and other media. Many did not know or couldn't believe that such terrible things had been happening for some time already. America and Great Britain were slow and uneasy in coming to aid; nevertheless, they eventually did.

One way help arrived was in the form of smuggling people to safety who were being persecuted, imprisoned, and tortured—sometimes across multiple borders. Smuggling a person from one country to another was not an easy task. It required complex logistical and financial planning along with thousands of hands to help those escaping the Nazi regime.

The women we will meet provided comfort and safety to those who couldn't find it in their usual places of worship or family support. Help was given to the people who didn't feel safe in their own skin anymore—never mind their hometown—and to parents who had to let go of their children and hope the children remembered who they were and what faith they were born into after the war ended.

Some achieved these rescues without the backing of an organization, but many worked together, which was also risky as Nazis could more easily infiltrate and uncover cooperative efforts. The main concern for the brave people smuggling refugees was whether they could keep fleeing families together or whether they had to split them up and rename them. Could they just walk across the border, or did they need to sneak through and pray for the best? Oftentimes, the answer was uncertain.

The Nazis knew how much Jewish communities valued their families and traditions and they used that to their advantage by removing anyone who believed or sympathized with such values. The Nazi regime members were smart, sly, and resourceful, which meant that rescuers and smugglers needed to be smarter still.

If someone did not look the part of "a law-abiding citizen," then they were ostracized. Male Jews usually wore a beard, their kippah or yarmulke (traditional skullcap) on their heads, and sometimes spoke in a heavy Yiddish accent. Nazis believed they could spot a Jew by just looking for the dark features and hooked noses, which were exaggerated ethnic stereotypes dating back as far as the 13th century.

JUDE was scratched on the walls and doors of houses and businesses. Beatings in the street and arrests in the middle of the night were not just a warning to Jews, but to underground resistance members, partisan fighters, sympathizers, and rescuers alike. It was therefore not just the Jews who ran for the hills, but anyone who stood in the way of the "sacrosanct Aryan ideals," such as anti-Nazis, political refugees, or principled gentiles (non-Jewish) who feared for their lives.

For most citizens of the Allied nations, the end of the Second World War was a happy event, celebrated with great jubilation, but for many others, it never truly ended. It remained an open wound for those who remembered being taken away from their parents and handed over to utter strangers, for those who stopped practicing Judaism because their circumstances prevented it, and for those who were released from the concentration and Prisoner of War (POW) camps, questioning their right to survive and wondering how they made it out alive.

For them, and for many others who suffered, it is a trauma that has never healed.

The injustices committed during WWII stripped people of their possessions, homes, lifestyles, spouses, children, parents, friends, religious practices, and livelihoods. Many millions of people lost their very lives.

What should not be lost is the honor and legacy of brave female heroes who were defamed or omitted from history books because of their gender, religion, and secret involvement in the war. Only recently, through letters, memoirs, and the declassification of formerly secret official documents, has society been given a real glimpse at the variety of ways in which brave women changed the course of World War II.

Our Heroes

Women in the 1930s and '40s were not passive, although history would have us believe this is to be so. They were often portrayed as victims in need of rescue, and so even when that wasn't the case, their achievements were overshadowed by their male counterparts, such as Oskar Schindler and Nicholas Winton, who received much of the publicity, credit, and glory.

This book reverses that paradigm and brings to light the brave female rescuers from across Europe and America, who actively risked their own lives to save others, often in appalling and dangerous conditions. As the book unfolds, each chapter reveals something new and valuable about their singular and collaborative efforts.

Peppered throughout the historical backdrop are pieces of the rescuers' stories that were influenced by films, books, interviews, and even imagination. We can't know everything these brave women did and thought, so occasional liberties are taken to fill out their stories, all in keeping with what is known of their lives and personalities.

- In **Chapter 1** we meet **Louise** and **Ida Cook**, sisters from **Great Britain** who might seem ordinary at first glance, but who turn out to be brilliant at turning this to their advantage to evade suspicion and save lives.

- In **Chapter 2** we encounter **Cecilia Razovsky** from **America**, a strong Jewish woman who fought tooth and nail for immigrants and refugees and never gave up actively campaigning for her fellow people.

- In **Chapter 3** we learn all about **Irena Sendler** from **Poland**—a Catholic woman who believed in the universality of human value, regardless of religion or race, and risked everything to smuggle children out of the Warsaw Ghetto.

- In **Chapter 4 Ebba Lund** from **Denmark** comes onto the scene to help her fellow citizens escape Nazi-occupied Denmark via fishing boats to safety in Sweden. Her kind heart and sharp mind proved they are the core qualifications for heroism.

- In **Chapter 5** we meet **Marie Schmolka** from **Czechoslovakia** and **Doreen Warriner** from **Great Britain.** These highly educated women were rendered almost invisible by the attention afforded to their male counterparts, but their deeds were paramount in the outcome of their famous rescue mission, the *Kindertransport*, which ferried thousands of children to safety.

- Finally, in **Chapter 6** we meet **Andrée de Jongh** from **Belgium**. This young woman's best disguise in smuggling fallen Allied airmen to safety via the Comet Line was her perceived innocence and diminutive stature.

What makes a hero? Louise, Irena, Ebba, Marie, and the others were not necessarily the strong, self-confident, athletic heroes we see in the movies. Some of them were small, shy, awkward, and unfashionable. Their stories prove that it is high time that popular perceptions of the very concept of heroism be challenged and become more inclusive.

Young and old, women were key rescuers and people smugglers who never ceased to motivate, involve, and support those around them. They tirelessly campaigned and put pressure on Allied governments to do more to help the refugees from Nazi-occupied countries and physically accompanied many to safer lands at their own risk.

What motivates a person to become a rescuer? Injustice, which we never seem to be lacking. Perhaps Ida, Cecilia, Doreen, and Andrée's courage and bravery will resound within you so that you hear their message loud and clear: Regardless of social status or physical prowess, anyone who decides to stand up for the courage of their convictions can become a rescuer.

Author Emma Werner writes about what it meant to be a rescuer in her book *A Conspiracy of Decency*: "Regardless of their nationality, social class, level of education, or religious and political persuasion, they shared one important characteristic. They defined their humanity by their ability to behave compassionately" (2004).

This was conceivably one of the darkest periods in history, which makes it all the more important to find and bring light to the sanity of compassion and kindness among the insanity of genocide and hate.

Before we begin, we must learn a bit about what made the enemy so strong and seemingly impregnable and how the German population came to believe in not just the ideals of power, but the *image of power* too. Nazi men and women performed some of the most gruesome and inhumane actions in the history of the war in the name of their Führer, and so I would like to detail some of the last things a captured Jew or refugee would see before their death: A uniform and a camp.

Nazi Uniforms

The power of a uniform lies in its silence. —Joseph Goebbels

Figure 2. Common peaked cap of the SS (Death Heads).

The notion of "image first" was always in Adolf Hitler's mind when he gained power in Germany in the early 1930s. He saw what the country had gone through and how their very identity was in question both at home and throughout the world. He couldn't tolerate this weakness. Germany needed definition, a rallying cry, and to command respect. It needed a total branding overhaul.

The uniform of Nazi Germany has been often called the most stylish uniform ever created—designed with intention and impeccably made. But there wasn't just a single uniform; there were actually several versions depending on service type and rank

If you were fleeing for your life, it was immensely important to know the differences in the uniform that your enemy wore and what that meant if you were captured. If you were a woman smuggling Jews, children, or sympathizers, you had to know who the enemy was and what the nuances of their uniforms meant.

The Germans were not shy to display their pride in their regime and found strength in the symbolism. In the early 1900s, the country adopted vivid colors, impressive headwear, and intricate designs as the unification of Germany was underway. Then when WWI arrived, they dulled it down by removing the frills and recognizable spiked helmets (*Pickelhaube*) for plain metal helmets *(Stahlhelm)*. This was done to project a unified image of the German army and to lessen costs for production under hyperinflation.

After WWI, Germany went through political change. Adolf Hitler arrived on the scene and took power under his Nazi Party. He wanted something clean, elegant, and powerful to propagate the Nazi sentiment. Now let me briefly point out some key differences in the Nazi officers' and soldiers' uniforms between 1935 and 1945.

The German Army was divided into the *Wehrmacht* (Army), the *Luftwaffe* (Air Force), and the *Kriegsmarine* (Navy). These uniforms were not much different from the uniforms of other Axis and Allied countries during WWII. They adopted the typical drab brown or gray-green color that was practical on the battlefield for comfort and disguise.

Hitler, on the other hand, had a special unit purposely under his devious control, the *Schutzstaffel* (directly translates to 'protection squadron') or better known as the *SS*. These men were not technically part of the military, but rather a paramilitary organization that answered only to Hitler.

The SS's well-known double lightning logo was a symbol of victory. They were further divided into three operations: (1) The **general SS**, who controlled and monitored Nazi regime operations; (2) the *Waffen-SS*, who were the armed foot soldiers fighting alongside Germany's military; and finally, (3) the **Deaths Head** units, who were in charge of the concentration camps.

The SS were truly iconic because their uniforms were fully black and tailored to fit perfectly. The hallmarks were the peak visor caps with the skull and crossbones badge (a sign of defying death), the high shiny boots, the neat white trimming, and the long jackets or gabardine capes were worn to demonstrate strength, mystery, fear, and control. One was meant to feel scared and uncomfortable when seeing the uniform— the silent threat of a well-groomed killer. Optimizing the black, white, and red color scheme was a brilliant contrast that defined the German army over those years and made them very visible. Visibility could instill fear.

A fourth subdivision of the SS was the infamous **Gestapo**, the secret police specifically charged with the extraction of Jewish communities. They wore a green-gray SS uniform instead of the traditional black, but often wore plain clothes to infiltrate groups and spy on unsuspecting victims.

It is sometimes misunderstood that the German company Hugo Boss designed *and* manufactured all the German uniforms during the war, but the company only manufactured them. SS officer Karl Diebitsch designed the look.

An obvious example of Nazi pride is seen in the Swastika used throughout the war. The design itself was taken from ancient times—a symbol of good luck, hope, and optimism. But when the Germans took it for their own, its meaning changed to the macabre symbol we know today as racist, genocidal, and antisemitic.

Additionally, the immense amount of propaganda issued at the time, mainly aimed at the German population, reinforced the message of power and unquestioning loyalty. Black and white films and photos brought great exposure to Nazi fashion and their intense discipline.

With that being said, the Nazi uniform reflected a far more subversive human aspect that its leaders, Adolf Hitler (short, dark, unassuming) and the SS commander Heinrich Himmler (weak, unmanly, shy), portrayed but condemned—that of inadequacy. The regime aimed to transcend the average human traits and become something of a god. But of course, the Nazis were just men who bled and cried, and like their uniforms, their pursuits became a shield to hide their flawed mortality.

Just imagine the fear a woman or man would experience at seeing one of those uniformed men walk around the corner in an occupied country, symbolizing a cog in a giant fascist machine that relentlessly pursued its victims.

If these women were going to go head-to-head with the regime and attempt to evade their watchful gaze, then they had to understand their enemy well, especially their uniforms and roles.

Nazi Camps

Arbeit Macht Frei (Work sets you free). —Infamous slogan on various concentration camp entrance gates.

Figure 3. Dachau main entrance gate.

The notorious image of a concentration camp entrance gate is something many of us are familiar with due to its ominous portrayal in movies and historical documentaries over the years. It remains a symbol of oppression.

The slogan tells us exactly what the intention of the camp is, and at the same time, it brings a sense of false hope to anyone who enters. We know that freedom only came *after* working oneself to *death*.

Today we think of concentration camps purely as a means of mass murder, but only towards the end of the war did many become camps for last-minute killings. Nazi camps initially had various names and purposes.

- Concentration camps (detention camps intended for "enemies of the Reich")
- Transit camps (holding camps used as a stop-off before transportation to killing centers)
- Prisoner of War (POW) camps (camps intended to house captured Allied and Soviet soldiers)
- Forced labor camps (camps designed for Jews and Gentiles to perform hard manual labor to fill economic shortages in Germany)
- Killing centers (euthanasia sites solely intended for mass killings).

You may have heard of the more infamous camps, such as the largest killing center Auschwitz-Birkenau (or simply Auschwitz), or Arbeitsdorf, the largest "work village" or labor camp along with Buchenwald, Dora, and Dachau. But, spread out across central Europe, the Nazis established sites in Germany, Poland, Austria, Czechoslovakia, France, and Belgium to name a few. In fact, "between 1933 and 1945, Nazi Germany and its allies established more than 44,000 camps and other incarceration sites (including ghettos)" (USHMM, 2009) around Europe.

The camps were under the control of the SS, as we now know, who were the core force under Hitler's thumb. SS officers managed the more nitty-gritty aspects of war, such as intelligence and infiltration within occupied governments and resistance organizations, but also the management of these camps.

One common misconception regarding the camps is that all arriving Jews or political refugees would receive the infamous five-, six-, or seven-digit number roughly tattooed on their left forearm. This procedure was only applied in the Auschwitz camp after 1941 when there was a large influx of Soviet soldiers and Nazis needed to easily identify the dead. The badges and armbands on clothing made it harder to accurately identify corpses whose clothes had been removed.

The badge we are so familiar with today, the yellow Jewish Star of David, was a combination of two triangles, not a five-point star. One triangle is upright with another inverted triangle placed over it. The star was intended to specifically identify the Jews, but it was often accompanied by other badges too. The most common badge was the invented triangle of various colors (each color represented the reason the person was in the camp) and sometimes letters (to represent special skills like translation or medicine).

Many who arrived at Auschwitz, for example, would never receive the tattoo or badge as they were sent directly from the train to the gas chambers. And if they did receive their number and designation, they had to sew it onto their own clothes upon arrival.

The well-known, blue-striped pattern on prisoner uniforms was not issued to all prisoners in all camps. The majority just had plain brown outfits with hats and shoes, and if you had a special skill or were "of importance" in the camp, then you had privileges, like warmer clothing, pockets, and cutlery.

Having said all of this, it is important to remember that it was not just men who controlled these camps, but women too. Female SS guards ran the women's sections of the camps and treated prisoners equally as brutally as the male guards.

The kind, gentle, and caring female image is turned on its head when we look at some of the female SS guards, such as Anneliese Kohlmann and Irma Grese (the Hyena of Auschwitz) who were as equally (or even more) sadistic and torturous than their male counterparts. A major concern after the war was the lack of punishment (especially seen with Kohlmann) of female SS officers. Their womanhood excused many from being held accountable for actions and it ultimately allowed some of them to walk free.

The World Jewish Congress and the American Congress compiled the final figure of deaths to be over 6 million people and "more than 1,000,000 of the 6,000,000 Jews exterminated by the Nazis in World War II were children under age fifteen" (Friedman, 1973).

It is much harder to love others and spread hope for and engender trust in humanity than it is to swim against the tide of violence, hatred, and greed. So without further ado, let us begin to look at the lives of the women featured in this book who chose this harder path; let us learn how they changed thousands of lives in the process.

Chapter 1

Louise & Ida Cook:

The Secretive Sisters

Figure 4. Ida & Louise Cook on the eve of their trip to New York, 1926. Photograph reproduced by kind

permission of the Estate of Ida Cook and Rupert Crew Limited © Victoria and Albert Museum, London.

If ever there were two women who could use their underestimated and plain female personas to bamboozle arrogant men, then Louise and Ida Cook were the women for the job.

These sisters conned the Nazi system with grace and guts at a time when many women were not the adventurous characters they read about in their novels. Louise and Ida, however, took a page straight out of the Scarlet Pimpernel in their secret mission to save lives during the Nazi reign of terror.

The Cook sisters played the international agenda to the tee, ensuring that the bureaucratic and inhumane policies surrounding refugee immigration to Great Britain were challenged. If the government proved to be ineffective, then the women took matters into their own hands.

The Threshold

Our story begins at the end of one century and the beginning of another. In Great Britain in 1901, Mary Louise Cook opened her eyes for the first time and soon became a vivacious little girl. Three years later, in 1904, she was joined by a baby sister, Ida. Two younger brothers, Bill and Jim, would follow in the years to come.

While the eldest, Louise, was known as the blushing beauty, Ida did not retain as many of her mother's softer features and was often teased endearingly as the ugly duckling. But God forbid anyone except her father tell that joke!

As their father was a customs official, he moved the family around often, which meant that the four siblings were brought up all around Britain. The Cook family was said to be a good-natured, level-headed, loving, and respectable English family. The arrival of the Great Depression after WWI (1914–1918) and the subsequent economic crash in the British Isles caused food shortages, diseases, and unemployment to spread like wildfire. The Cook family proved to be practical and self-reliant, but the turmoil affected millions of families in those years between wars.

The couple loved their brood and never missed an opportunity to instill vital values in their impressionable children along the way, such as compassion and gratitude. Both girls attended Duchess Girls' School in the iconic town of Alnwick (where the noted Alnwick Castle is located), and in later years they shared an apartment in London where they worked as typists in the Civil Service.

From One Passion to the Next

The two women loved nothing more than going to the opera. As they grew up in the 1920s and 1930s, they developed a passion for the European operatic greats and often traveled into occupied territory to watch their favorite performances.

They befriended Romanian soprano Viorica Ursuleac and her famous Austrian fiancé, the conductor Austrian Clemens Krauss. Krauss would become instrumental in veering the sisters away from the passive sentiment of "we hope this war ends soon" to the proactive and humanitarian sentiment of "we need to help as many as we can get through this war."

Their favorite composer was Puccini, and the sisters also became close friends with Italian opera composers and singers alike. Their nephew, John Cook, in later years would call his two aunts "opera groupies" (*The opera-loving sisters*, 2017) as a loving reminder of their absolute obsession with the art.

By 1933, the National Socialist German Workers Party (Nazis), headed by their peculiar leader Adolf Hitler, was putting more and more pressure on German and Austrian Jews, causing them to flee for their lives at the first opportunity they got.

But fleeing became difficult because the Nazis imposed all kinds of bureaucratic blockages, not only on the German and Austrian Jews, but also on democratic and communist politicians as well as sympathizers. Party officials denied Western visas and placed restrictions that put Jews and sympathizers in dire straits. The *Kindertransport* operation (to be explored in Chapter 5) was established in 1938 to help many children escape, but many adults had nowhere to go—even if they had money and status.

Bribery was ineffective as the Nazis took everything they owned anyway. Jews needed to come up with plans to stow their valuable belongings *before* they were taken away. Later, they could figure out how to extract themselves from the regime's tight grip.

Families begged their prominent friends for help, and those prominent friends spoke to other friends in safer countries, such as England and America. That is how the rescue operation ball started rolling.

At the time, the Cook sisters were in their 30s, unmarried, and living an ordinary, quiet life. People made presumptions about any woman of that age without a husband or children; they were often labeled spinsters or rather eccentric. But the sisters worked hard, and because they scrimped and saved in their earlier years to buy airline tickets to the newest opera, they began to travel somewhat frequently. Air travel became their hook into the rescue operation.

Historians find this fact to be very surprising considering that plane fares were very expensive in the early years of commercial flight. How these two sisters managed to scrape together enough money to make these trips is astonishing. But thanks to the Cook sisters' frequent trips to European cities and the countryside, and their willing partners there, they were able to do something truly significant, albeit extremely dangerous.

In 1934, the Cook sisters traveled to Salzburg, a city on the Austrian-German border in the Alps, to attend the yearly opera festival. The two were almost completely oblivious to the fear and foreboding that was silently playing out around them.

Due to their international friendships and their pursuit of the arts, they were encouraged to become more than fans and friends, but helpers to the Austrian conductor's Jewish friends. Interestingly enough, Clemens Krauss was a member of the Nazi party and would have been shot dead if discovered helping Jews escape. It was always nice to find Germans and Austrians in secret sympathy with Jews and sympathizers who were willing to stand up for them.

The Move

"Her name is Frau Mitia Mayer-Lismann," Krauss said to the two sisters staring up at him. Ida and Louise looked at each other then back at him, unsure of how to respond to such a request after an otherwise vibrant performance.

"Clemens, why do you need us to accompany her back to London with us? Not that we mind, of course, but she is a grown woman, isn't she?" asked Ida.

"Yes, she is. But we are hearing frightful stories of Jewish people being harassed upon leaving Austria, and some have been disappearing when they leave the country or travel anywhere at all. I am worried for her."

Krauss sighed heavily, looking depressed. "Just stay close; maybe take her out to see the London sights. It is a short trip after all, and I would truly be so grateful!" he pleaded with tears in his eyes.

Of course, they would help. It was such a small thing, to watch out for Mitia, and so they did. The three women flew back to London together, and the sisters showed her around the city. What they weren't expecting to hear was that this was Frau Mayer-Lismann's official escape and that she was not planning on flying back to Europe until the political climate changed.

In her 1950 memoir, *We Followed Our Stars*, later republished as *Safe Passage*, Ida Cook recalls how that conversation with the Jewish woman struck a chord within her and molded her and her sister's future. She wrote (Miller, 2017):

> We began to see things more clearly and to see them, to our lasting benefit, through the eyes of an ordinary devoted family like ourselves. By the time the full horror of what was happening in Germany, and later in Austria, reached the newspaper, the whole thing had become almost too fantastic for the ordinary mind to take in.

Over the next year, they began making contacts with people in London and asserting their understanding of the mission they wanted to take on, but it required a lot more than just talking and hoping; it required hard work and ample funding.

Risky Flights

Around 1936 the younger sister, Ida Cook, discovered her passion for writing. She started publishing daring and adventurous romance novels under the pseudonym of Mary Burchell for the publishing house Mills & Boon, and then later, Harlequin. Her books became very popular, which helped fund lodging and passage (air or boat tickets) and pledges of safety for those rescued.

"We began to coordinate the smaller offers of money or hospitality around individual cases until we had enough money or hospitality to "cover a case." writes Ida. "Then we would persuade some trusting friend or relative to sign the official guarantee form, on the understanding that the guarantee would never be called on because we already had the wherewithal to meet the needs of the case" (Miller, 2017).

But when their own money was running low, the sisters only became more daring and resourceful. Their unassuming manner was perfect for what they were tasked to do. Getting the right immigration papers to be filed in Britain required a good sum of money from the Jewish person (Miller, 2017):

> Jewish refugees had to be sponsored by a British citizen or they had to produce a large sum of money guaranteeing they wouldn't be a burden on the state. Because refugees were not allowed to work in Britain, this financial

guarantee had to be produced upfront, posing a near-insurmountable burden on many Jews.

If Jews couldn't travel with their belongings, then they couldn't secure the funds for visas and lodging, which meant that many were stuck. How were those fleeing going to get the money needed to ensure their papers were approved by Britain so that they could fly or sail there legally?

Enter the Cook sisters. Their ability to travel through customs and security checks with money and valuables on their person with relative ease made them just the people to fool guards and inspectors. Plus, their cover story—opera fanaticism—was real.

For a good four years, the sisters traveled to and from England on their secret missions, ensuring the British government approved their emigration papers. Every three months or so they would purchase airfares to less popular airports to avoid scrutiny. They flew out on a Friday, met with the refugee, took their information or their valuables, attended an opera or two, and then caught a boat back to Britain on Sunday—just in time to start their working week at their typewriters on Monday! Interestingly, when these two women traveled, they traveled cheaply. But when they arrived, they stayed in the most luxurious German and Austrian hotels and attended the most popular opera houses, brushing shoulders with the likes of Heinrich Himmler (Holocaust architect), Hermann Goering (major military leader), and Joseph Goebbels (Minister of propaganda), to name a few.

The sisters understood German and were able to listen in on conversations between Nazi leaders (who assumed their words were spoken in total confidence), which could be passed on to British leadership. The Cooks were not just smugglers, but spies too, and their involvement during those years was probably much more in-depth than they revealed.

Potential refugees gave the sisters everything they had in the world to purchase their freedom, including strings of pearls, heavy diamond earrings, bulky rings, expensive fur coats, and of course, cash. The tricky thing was that if the sisters arrived in the country with a bag each, but left with more than double, it would be highly suspect. To minimize bulk, the sisters would wear the jewelry and clothes and hide the money as deep into their pockets and bags as they could. While this generally worked smoothly, they did have their fair share of scares when they thought they'd be caught. They knew that if they were, they might never see home again.

***

The Austrian officer stared at Louise as she and her sister were in the queue awaiting inspections at the border to return home. He looked her up and down and then gestured with his finger for her to move out of the line and come forward.

Her heart stopped.

"Pass over your papers and tell me, what was your reason for visiting?" He spoke sternly, expecting a quick and honest response. She quickly handed over her identification.

I mustn't panic, she thought. She answered in decent-enough German and explained that she was a huge opera fan, pulling pamphlets out of her pockets to prove her story. But the officer wasn't convinced.

"Frau Cook, how does it come about that you are wearing the most impressive pearls around your neck, while dressed in such shabby clothing. Are those your pearls? Explain yourself at once!"

It was time to change tactics and adopt "our nervous British spinster act," huffing and puffing as if put off by the personal affront (Cook, 2008).

"To comment on the quality of my outfit in public! I've never been so offended in all my life!" she responded indignantly, almost tearfully.

She proceeded to mumble that she didn't trust her family not to steal from her, so she needed to travel with her favorite jewelry. This made the officer uncomfortable enough to dismiss her. The scheme worked like a charm, and she dabbed at her eyes and joined her sister in the remaining queue, her handkerchief hiding the slightest smile.

When the two women were home, they didn't stop for a minute. During the day, they worked full-time jobs, but at night and in their free time, they spoke to people, imploring assistance and pledging around London for incoming refugees. The two of them even bought a flat in London specifically for refugees who were transitioning to life in England.

Ida was particularly vocal and forthright about the Jewish situation in Europe, and she spoke to anyone who would listen. The local news simply wasn't covering enough of the horrors occurring throughout Germany and Poland for people to truly understand. To make matters worse, the immigration policies were inconceivably unaccommodating.

Ida was invited to speak at a refugee and immigration policy conference. She became infuriated by the men who spoke before her. They were disillusioned and uncommitted to the truth at hand. When it was her turn to speak, she got straight to the point and described a recent request of a Jewish man desperate to leave Nazi-occupied territory (Miller, 2017):

> He has asked me to save his life. He is under sentence to go to Buchenwald Concentration camp – and almost certain death – unless he can be got out of the country in a matter of weeks. I have no guarantee. I have no means of saving him. He must die unless I can find both, and find them quickly.

Over the course of five years of undercover work, Ida and Louise Cook managed to smuggle a total of 29 documented people out of Europe and into Britain. It is estimated that there are dozens more who managed to evade imprisonment and death thanks to their financial assistance and guidance.

Jewish photographer Lisa Basch was the last person the sisters rescued out of Europe in 1939. Louise was overwhelmed with work, so Ida alone traveled to Germany to find the 25-year-old woman and interview her for the request of a guarantee to Britain. Basch's home in Frankfurt had been destroyed and she was alone, as her family and friends had already evacuated.

Those years were certainly quite crazy and surrounded by urgency, yet Ida Cook later writes: "The funny thing is, we weren't the James Bond type—we were just respectable Civil Service typists" (Cook, 2008).

The Close

By the end of 1939, there wasn't much a person could do internationally to help as the war had officially begun and bombs were about to fly. But what the Cook sisters did over the preceding four years was everything to the women and children who had been saved.

The Cook sisters carried on with whatever help they could give from back home during the war years, but what was truly needed to save everyone was much more than any two people could give. They moved around for some time, visiting and staying in various countries, but eventually returned to their homeland of England.

Lisa Basch spoke to the *Daily Telegraph* in 2007 remembering the two women fondly. She mentioned how Ida was a mother figure to her during that time, and that when the two women moved to New York later in their lives, Ida stayed with Lisa for some time. Lisa said, "I was completely at their service, wherever they had to go, whomever they wanted to visit, I drove them there." Lisa recalled that Ida told her that she had nothing to repay, but Lisa responded that she wanted to regardless. "I was so grateful. I loved her really" (Miller, 2017).

Ida published her memoir, *We Followed Our Stars,* in 1950. The sisters were brought into the spotlight in 1956, specifically Ida, to make a surprise appearance on *This is Your Life*, a British television production that documented her life and achievements for the world to see.

In 1965, the two sisters were honored by the Yad Vashem Martyrs and Heroes Remembrance Authority in Israel as Righteous Among the Nations.

The younger of the two sisters, Ida, passed away first in 1986, while Louise followed her in 1991. They didn't leave immediate family, but their legacy still speaks volumes through their well-lived lives. Ida's memoir, *We Followed Our Stars,* was expanded and retitled in 2008 to *Safe Passage*.

A plaque was erected by Sunderland Council in Sunderland (where the sisters lived for some time) in 2017, commemorating their immense role in history.

The curator commented: "This blue plaque provides us with a great opportunity to raise awareness of these remarkable ladies and their remarkable bravery during the darkest days in history" (*Sunderland's honoured*, 2016).

A feature film is reportedly underway, titled *The Cooks*, starring Emma Thompson as one of the sisters. Hopefully, the portrayal of their adventure is adapted accurately and highlights the sisters' love for each other and others, never forgetting their subtle British humor.

The story of the Cook sisters illustrates how we can find real heroes in the unlikeliest of people. While their inner strength and courage were not always visible, their legacy surely proves that any one of us has the potential to be a hero. You don't have to look or even act the part to be brave and change people's lives for the better.

Author Mari Eder wrote a chapter in her 2021 book, *The Girls Who Stepped Out of Line*, about the courageous story of the two women, mentioning that they were fully aware that their appearance was "nothing special, nothing memorable. It was what made them so successful in a risky, illegal, and dangerous business" (Eder, 2021).

Their ingenious method of evasion and true passion to fight for humanitarian values shows us that these two women made their ordinary lives extraordinary and accomplished some incredibly memorable deeds.

Chapter 2:

Cecilia Razovsky: Saving Her Own

Figure 5. Cecilia Razovsky (center) Photo courtesy of the American Jewish Historical Society, from the Papers of Cecilia Razovsky (P-290), Box 7, Folder 20.

Cecilia Razovsky, our next female rescuer, was herself an American Jew and a fierce campaigner for human rights. Although she lived far from the war, she remained close to the action. Her story steers us straight into American immigration policy, which due to immense economic stress and unjustified emigration fears, was its own tangle of dubious inaction.

What would have been the Jewish death count had the Allied nations done more, and done it sooner? If they had only opened their eyes to the warning signs and paid attention to the alarm bells sounding in Europe, especially surrounding the mass exodus of European Jews to the US and Britain, then maybe the war would have gone differently.

Cecilia Razovsky, a patriot passionate about immigration, offered a voice and a helping hand to refugees who needed to flee. She fought for Child Labor laws and Americanization (a belief that immigrants can assimilate smoothly into American customs) throughout her life in pursuit of bringing people together.

As we look into the life of this unassuming Jewish woman with immensely intelligent eyes and an intellect to match, we see that she found herself in a place where her choices and actions could directly affect the relationship between countries and people. She used that to her advantage and helped to save thousands of lives in the process.

Like the Cook sisters, this rescuer primarily operated from the safety of a free, unoccupied country. Unlike most, Razovsky saw what was to come and understood what needed to be done. This proactive woman took the reins and put her life in danger by traveling to

Germany alone. Her story begs the question: How many more Jewish women, forgotten by history, were also rescuers?

The Threshold

To enter this story, we must venture to the turn of the 19th century. Cecilia Davidson Razovsky was born in 1891 in St. Louis, Missouri, in Midwestern America. Her parents, Minna and Jonas, were Russian immigrants who moved to America for a so-called better life. Here we find the Razovsky family, very poor, living in a small ghetto, and holding on tight to their Jewish faith. They had bought into the American dream and firmly believed that hard work would get them there—no matter the cost.

Consequently, at the age of 12, Razovsky began working in a sweatshop sewing buttons on shirts and doing anything to help the family stay afloat. During those formative childhood years, she worked many other jobs, such as waitress, secretary, and salesgirl.

Today it is hard to turn away from the image of a child doing labor, but well over a hundred years ago, it wasn't uncommon for children to labor alongside their parents. It was a sacrifice everyone had to be willing to make in order to get by.

This combined family effort to make it through life somehow had a positive impact on the young girl, who at age 20 started teaching English to Jewish immigrants at the Jewish Educational Alliance in her hometown of St. Louis. She did this for the next six years.

Despite not being able to play with other children and go to school as a child, Razovsky received some incredibly vital life lessons from working. Being from an immigrant family herself, the first lesson she learned was that she needed to help other mothers, fathers, and children coming from Europe to America. She understood that speaking, walking, and looking like an American was the fastest way to start making a life for any immigrant. To be treated "just like everybody else" in America during those fragile years, you had to make yourself look and act just like them.

The second lesson was that she would not stand for the American government's acceptance of immigrant children, or any children, into the labor force. Times were changing and the workforce needed to change with it. She had experienced that life for herself and decided she wasn't going to stand idly by and watch others send their children to work. Children needed to learn from books, not labor.

Razovsky also understood that education was the key tool for her to be heard and recognized, so while she worked, she never stopped studying. In 1911, she attended Washington University in St. Louis and then moved to Corliss School of Law the following year. In 1913, she attended the St. Louis School of Economics followed by the Chicago School of Civics and Philanthropy in 1919 after a job in Washington, DC.

During all of these years of higher education, Razovsky also served as an attendance officer on the Board of Education in St. Louis, chairperson at the Cruden Center (a suffrage organization in public voting), and on the board of the Business Women's Equal Suffrage League (which she helped found too).

With all of these achievements under her belt, it's no wonder that the federal government cherry-picked her to work with them in Washington DC.

The Move

When Razovsky turned 26 in 1917, she moved to Washington DC to work at the United States Children's Bureau as an inspector where she earned $2,120 a year. There she was enveloped in the world of social reform; she stayed until 1920.

In the 2008 book, *Cecilia Razovsky and the American Jewish Women's Rescue Operations in the Second World War*, author Bat-Ami Zucker explains the power Razovsky wielded during these earlier years under the National Committee saying: "Razovsky was in charge of enormous projects, dealing not only with assisting immigrants already in the United States but also with assisting for immigration from Europe. Her work was highly appreciated in Washington" (Zucker, 2008).

The National Child Labor Committee's goal was to emphasize the repercussions of using children under age 16 for labor-intensive work. The only way to change the country's mind was to show evidence of the egregious labor conditions and the atrocities being committed daily. Razovsky played an important part in leading "outrage campaigns." by sending leaflets and mass mail to communities with pictures of children, locals, and refugees, doing harsh manual labor and living in poverty.

In the early 1900s, many laws restricting child labor were passed as part of the progressive reform movement of this period, yet many southern US states firmly resisted the change, insisting that they instead adhere to the federal child labor law that allowed them to employ children.

Razovsky's main interest was convincing the public that school was more important than work and that by adhering to minimum wages and a required amount of school attendance, the nation would slowly but surely veer away from needing underage labor. Still, "many of these laws were full of loopholes that were readily exploited by employers hungry for cheap labor" (*Child labor*, 2009).

As an inspector, she was required to conduct surveys and study the field, and as a result, her interest in social welfare skyrocketed with the increase in immigration laws between Europe and America. Secretary of Labor, Francis Perkins, listed Razovsky as an expert in the Ellis Island immigration surveys, where she monitored whether foreigners were mentally and physically healthy to work and live in America. The conditions on the island were unsanitary, crowded, and dark, and many suffered from trachoma, a very contagious eye infection that could easily cause blindness.

When the Supreme Court disbanded the Child Labor Division in 1918, Razovsky returned to Chicago to finish her studies in sociology, but never stopped working within the welfare and immigration department.

Razovsky joined the National Council of Jewish Women (NCJW) in 1921 and became the Executive Secretary of the Department of Immigrant Aid that same year. With the NCJW, she was able to do some of her most compelling work as the editor for their magazine, *The Immigrant*, in which she published many articles offering guidance for newly immigrated women (many Jewish) arriving in foreign lands. Her most prominent works were: "What Every Immigrant Should Know" (1922), "What Every Woman Should Know About Citizenship" (1926), "Handicaps in Naturalization" (1932), and "Making Americans" (1938).

In 1927, Razovsky married Morris Davidson, a doctor with whom she had one son named David L. Davidson. She accomplished so much over the next years of her life that one can only wonder how she managed to juggle motherhood with her career and convictions.

A Mouthpiece for Children

Finally! Something big, Razovsky thought to herself as she got ready to board a plane to Vienna.

It was 1932, and she was well on her way to becoming a voice of reason and a paragon of steadfast action in the talks of Jewish emigration policies. She was sent to Austria to sit as a delegate for the NCJW at the First World Congress of Jewish Women. Women from all over the world came together for the very first time to talk about homelessness, refugees, concerns about Palestinian support, and the role of Jewish women in the community.

The period between 1929 and 1939, the Great Depression, was a time of immense fear. Thousands of American citizens were jobless; therefore, President Roosevelt introduced the New Deal, which aimed to remove children from the workplace, thus creating more jobs for adults to ignite the US economy once more. But sadly, the threat of war and the overwhelming number of refugees overshadowed the New Deal.

When it was Razovsky's turn to stand up and speak in Vienna, she said (Danty, n.d.):

> I feel like I am fighting our entire governmental structure. I am appalled by the anti-Semitic rubbish of (Father) Coughlin and others. How can Roosevelt and his advisors fear that a few children, Jewish Children, will ruin the 'New

Deal,' take food out of the mouths of others and be a burden on our society? All this happens as I know that every day more and more are sent to concentration camps and death. I cannot take even one moment to rest.

Razovsky was part of various groups geared to pressure President Roosevelt to find a better solution for the refugees and increase the immigration quotas. Without assistance from the government, many citizens took it into their own hands to sneak people into America (Zucker, 2021):

> Razovsky operated simultaneously on two fronts. She established contact with the *Hilfsverein der Deutschen Juden*, the Berlin-based Jewish organization that was in charge of locating and choosing the children, as well as delivering the relevant documents to the main office in New York.

Razovsky had been working closely with Secretary of Labor Perkins, who was the first woman ever to serve in a presidential cabinet. Like President Roosevelt, Perkins was a democrat, and in her position, she was also responsible for many of the new jobs given to women when men left the country for war.

Together, Perkins and Razovsky advocated for the plight of Jewish children fleeing to America (during both wars). Razovsky created the German-Jewish Children's Aid (GJCA) to assist unaccompanied refugee children in America and "to guarantee that the children would not become a public charge, the GJCA opened a bank account of $27,000" (Zucker, 2021). With the help of Perkins, the organization managed to assist the first group of 250 children to arrive in New York in 1934.

Immigration and labor departments around the world were strained when the antisemitic Nuremberg Laws were signed in 1935 and then implemented. Under the Nazi government, Jewish communities were permanently and violently displaced. These new laws precluded Jewish citizens from keeping their normal jobs and living their normal lives. They were prevented from traveling, marrying non-Jewish citizens, entering certain premises, and working certain jobs.

The catalyst for the mass exodus of Jews was the unprecedented violence of the *Kristallnacht* (night of the broken glass, due to the many smashed windows) in 1938, when Nazi officers and Hitler Youth members destroyed, ransacked, and burned thousands of Jewish homes, businesses, and synagogues arresting "nearly 30,000 Jewish men and boys, sending them to concentrations camps" throughout Germany and surrounding regions (USHMM, 2019b).

Prior to the war, Germany had over 500,000 Jewish citizens, but when the Nazi regime took hold, more than 300,000 of them fled, fearing they'd be captured or worse (USHMM, 2019b).

Being Kind

"I don't want to stay here! I miss Mommy!" cried the eleven-year-old boy in Hebrew as he looked up at Razovsky with teary eyes.

"I know, my darling," she said softly as she knelt beside him. "But you have to be strong and brave because your parents love you and want you to be safe." This was a reassuring statement that she had said over and over again, despite not being able to fully promise children's reunion with their parents. She glanced over at the foster mother.

"This is all too much for me, Cecilia. He cries all day, and it breaks my heart that we cannot ease his troubles. Please help," said the foster mother standing behind her as she looked at the boy with tenderness.

Of course she would help. Razovsky not only assisted in the logistical support to find housing for these children, but also the emotional support they needed to get through the first year without their parents in a new land and with a new language.

Although homes, foster families, food, and schooling were given to these immigrant children (aged two to sixteen), that was simply not enough to quench the children's true need for their families. So Razovsky kept an eye out for all the children struggling to adjust, usually the younger ones, sometimes taking them home with her and talking to them, and sometimes scheduling therapy sessions for them.

It must have been very hard to see and hear the trauma of these Jewish children who didn't fully understand what was going on but who felt all the anxiety and fear from the adults around them all the same.

Between 1923 and 1937 Razovsky would take the opportunity to travel the world in pursuit of helping refugees. In 1923, and again in 1935, she visited European port cities to establish emigration papers; the latter trip to Germany was quite dangerous. She also traveled to Cuba in 1924 to assess refugee camps there. The capital, Havana, had become a prime hub for WWII refugees fleeing Germany by boat, as did many other Allied Caribbean countries. Their legislation was more accommodating, and their governments accepted refugees more readily.

She also traveled to Canada in 1926, Mexico in 1930, and Argentina and Brazil in 1937 in her pursuit to assist their plight. Her husband joined her on many of these trips, and when the stay was prolonged, they brought their son with them.

Razovsky began working under the Coordination Committee of Refugee Resettlement, which in 1939 changed its name to the National Refugee Service. The big questions the highest officials in Western governments were asking were: Where do we take all these Jewish refugees? How do we support these displaced people in Germany? How do we avoid further stressing the economy?

America and Great Britain had a crisis on their hands.

American President Roosevelt commissioned a conference in July of 1938 to address the mass exodus of people from European countries. Representatives from 32 nations convened in the town of Évian, which would be known as the Évian Conference. The willingness of the majority of these nations, including Canada, Australia, and France, to accept the refugees was teetering on repudiation, with only the Dominican Republic openly accepting the larger influx of Europeans.

The US was overwhelmed with visa applications with only 27,000 available positions in the face of the 300,000 applicants (USHMM, 2019b). Germans, Czechoslovakians, and Austrians requested sanctuary, but many were refuted and sent back into the horrors of Europe.

The giant backlash from citizens across the US was piqued by the handling of the *MS St. Louis*. The ship was carrying over 900 refugees who had sailed from Hamburg to Cuba only to be sent back to Europe that next day because Cuba, the US, and Canada denied entry to the refugees. Even with the help of England, France, the Netherlands, and Belgium accepting a portion of the people, some 600 Jews were returned to occupied Europe, and of those 600, almost 300 were never seen again.

Between 1944 and 1948 Razovsky worked with the United Nations Relief and Rehabilitation Administration as well as the American Jewish Joint Distribution Committee.

Among the many organizations we have previously mentioned, Razovsky also stood at German Children's Aid, the United Service for New Americans, the Citizens Committee on Displaced Persons, and the Hebrew Immigration Aid Society Service. She was described as "arguably the single individual most responsible for the 1,000 children who found a safe haven in the United States" (Danty, n.d.). She became a beacon of hope for many parents who had lost so much.

The Close

Cecilia Razovsky would go on to say in her later years, "It is my sacred duty to rescue our Jewish Children and bring them to safety" (Danty, n.d.). Something she did with every breath of every day.

In 1957, she moved to Texas to be closer to the border between USA and Mexico, as she was very involved in the South American Resettlement, and became supervisor of the operation. Razovsky's family later moved to Brazil, and lastly settled in California.

The 73-year-old eventually decided to retire from her labor and immigration work in 1964. Razovsky still loved to write, and for the last four years of her life, she would compile memories and journals on her personal and professional insight into a changing world after WWII.

Razovsky died in 1968 in San Diego, California.

What can we say about dear Cecilia Razovsky Davidson? She was extremely dedicated and possessed an unparalleled strength of character. She pursued her goals with incredible determination and drive. But we also honor her compassion—not just for her Jewish kin, but for people who were at risk, lost, confused, and needing help to move on with their lives in peace.

Her work was her life, and with or without the backing of prominent Jewish organizations, she managed to assist by understanding the immigration system well enough to navigate it with ease.

Looking back, we are now aware of the consequences of poor bureaucratic decisions at state and national levels during WWII, but should we excuse the fact that these countries' leaders put their economic fears above the lives of Jewish immigrants? Should we look down on US and British citizens for xenophobic talk and actions? Can we honestly say that those sentiments are not still rampant today in their own way?

Cecilia saw fear in the world and countered it with love, dedication, and resilience.

Chapter 3:

Irena Sendler: The Good Catholic Smuggler

Figure 6. Irena Sendlerowa, 1942.

If we are to talk about moral fortitude, courage, and conviction, then we must collectively remember the story of Irena Sendler.

Unlike the previous women rescuers, Sendler carried out her rescue missions within one of the most dangerous arenas of war—occupied Poland, specifically the Warsaw ghetto.

Before being publicly recognized in the early 2000s by a Kansas high school project called Life in a Jar, Sendler's achievements, which had barely been appreciated in the first place, were all but forgotten. Yet her underground resistance network achieved an almost impossible feat: They rescued 2,500 Jewish children from the heavily-guarded Warsaw ghetto and hid them in safe houses around Poland.

We know that Hitler executed orders to invade Poland not long after his incursion in Czechoslovakia in 1939 and the onslaught on Poland was calculated and rigid. Yet, on behalf of young people who still had many years ahead of them, Irena Sendler and her underground compatriots would not stand for this injustice.

The Threshold

Irena Stanisława Krzyżanowska was born into a Catholic family in 1910 in the capital city of Warsaw, Poland.

Her family lived in the Jewish neighborhood of Otwock and were close friends with everyone, regardless of their faith. Irena's father, Dr. Stanisław Krzyżanowska, sympathized with the Jewish cause and often told his daughter: "A person must be rescued when drowning, regardless of religion or nationality" (TED-Ed, 2021).

This help is exactly what he provided to all those who couldn't afford medical care in the aftermath of WWI. The economic hardship brought on by the Great Depression was one issue, but an outbreak of typhus was another major problem during this period. Typhus is a bacterial infection that is often passed on by mites and ticks from infected animals to humans, and due to the severe lack of sanitation and proper healthcare at the time, many people succumbed to the disease well into WWII.

The doctor's proximity to hundreds of ill patients, and the fact that he was the only doctor who was willing to help the Jewish citizens in town, were most likely why he contracted the disease when Sendler was only seven years old. He died soon after.

As a Polish Catholic, Sendler was expected never to sympathize with the so-called "Jewish rats," as the Jewish community was being increasingly referred to, but because of her father's moral convictions, her view of humanity widened and evolved.

The Jewish community in Otwock was so grateful for the help that her father had given over the years that they offered to pay for Sendler's schooling in Warsaw, although her proud mother, Janina, kindly refused them. The two of them left Otwock after her father's death, stopping in other towns before settling in central Warsaw, where Sendler joined the Polish Democratic Youth Party (or *Związek Polskiej Młodzieży Demokratycznej*) and entered the University of Warsaw to study Polish literature and law.

In 1929, she started to show her first signs of defiance against a bigoted government's schemes of division. She had been studying for two years and was known to be outspoken about the Polish government's implementation of the segregation law, which needlessly separated Jewish and non-Jewish students within classrooms. In 1935, she was suspended from the university and then returned in 1937. Unfortunately, the political situation had not gotten any better.

At age 21, Irena married a Polish man named Mieczysław Sendler, but the couple never shared much of a loving relationship. A soldier deployed during the war, he was captured and remained a POW until liberation by Allied troops in 1945. The two never had children and divorced two years after the war.

Changing Mindsets

Starting in 1935, the Second Polish Republic began issuing its own antisemitic policies throughout Poland. One in particular forced Jewish students to sit on the left side of the auditorium or classroom in university buildings. Known as the "ghetto-benches," these segregated seating arrangements merely foreshadowed what the Nazis were to implement four years later.

When Sendler received her report card in 1937, she was surprised to see a large red stamp clearly indicating that she was of "non-Jewish origin."

How are my Jewish friends any different from me? she wondered. *They look, talk, and behave just like me. Why should we be separated?*

In protest, she started scratching out (defacing) the red stamp on her report card, challenging the new law, and telling her classmates and family, as well as her government, that antisemitic agendas were not something she tolerated.

"It's simply preposterous," Sendler said while waiting for the professor to arrive to lecture.

"You know Irena, I get it," said her college friend, Anna, who was sitting beside her, "but they have taken our jobs at a time when our people are desperate to get this country back to how it used to be!" She looked down sadly at her desk, fiddling with her books. "We need to be distinguishable from *them*," she said looking pointedly at the other side of the classroom where the Jewish students sat.

"That is not what inclusion under God means, Anna. It means we all are flesh and blood, and we can come together with understanding and respect. What happened to those ideals?"

"You are a voice of philosemitism, Irena. Be careful how loud you speak," said Anna in a cautionary yet vexed manner, quickly silencing herself as the professor entered the auditorium.

Irena knew that philosemitism is an interest in and respect for Jewish values and culture shown by someone who is not ethnically or culturally Jewish and she was proud of it. Because of her loud claims of liberty and human freedoms, Sendler would be suspended again from the university for some time before returning.

Over those years in school, she joined many different parties and organizations working on social welfare for women, children, and minorities in Warsaw. She became a member of the Free Polish University, surrounding herself with and being heavily influenced by the Communist Party of Poland, which was outlawed by the Polish government.

After that, she joined the Section of Mother and Child Assistance at the Citizen Committee for Helping the Unemployed, where she worked as a legal counselor and social worker and was able to help impoverished Jewish community members, especially women whose children were born out of wedlock. She published a couple of papers on the matter and was passionate about the subject.

Within her workplace, she made many important friendships, such as Professor Helena Radlińska and her fellow female students, who would assist her in her later heroic ventures. But due to increasing fascist ideals among government officials, in 1935 the committee was abolished, leaving most of the members to move to the Department of Social Welfare and Public Health.

Sendler graduated from university in September of 1939, just as the German and Soviet armies entered Poland in what came to be known as the September Campaign.

Initially, the Soviet Union was neutral to Germany's regime, but they were still invested in the "non-aggressive" possession of land, specifically that of Poland, their shared neighbor.

A few months prior to the invasion of Poland, Nazi Germany and the Soviet Union made a deal known as the Molotov-Ribbentrop Pact, which stipulated that they would annex the lands of Poland—Germany would take the west and the USSR would take the east.

The Polish army could not battle on both the eastern and western fronts, and the English were taking too long to come to their defense. As such, even without a formal surrender, Poland fell firmly into Nazi and Soviet hands a month later. Their alliance, strategy, and force were too great.

In the previous chapter, we came to understand the implications of a mass evacuation of millions of people from Europe on the rest of the world. The Poles were the first to feel the pressure and the last to hear the screams.

Thousands of people, the majority Jewish, scattered to neighboring countries and applied for visas to places as far away from the German whip as possible.

Working as a social worker in Warsaw was messy and challenging after 1939. During the previous year, Razovsky had worked side-by-side with her Polish acquaintances, her friends, and her appointed colleagues. Now, she was surrounded by black suits, black caps, shiny black boots, and unflinching stares. Everywhere she looked she saw the red, black, and white Swastika, and heard the sound of German commands on every corner.

Her Jewish friends and colleagues were removed from their workplaces and barely permitted to leave their homes. Nazi troops ransacked Jewish businesses and terrorized citizens. And this was only the beginning of the true terror to come.

Sendler joined the Polish Socialist Party (*Polska Partia Socjalistyczna* or PPS) that year, and being an activist and a volunteer nurse, she was already volunteering to help the injured Polish soldiers after their failed defense.

Along with her acquaintances—Irena Schultz, Jadwiga Sałek-Denekom, and Jadwiga Piotrowska—Sendler would falsify medical documents so that the Nazi officers would allow them to get the support they needed from the welfare organization.

As German troops marched in the streets looking at Jews with antipathy, Irena's many Jewish friends were fearing for their lives in their homes, unsure of what was going to happen next. A plan developed in her mind. Irena shared that plan, people agreed, and they helped. It was time to fight back!

The Move

Anyone who had two eyes and two ears knew that the large-scale construction of fences and checkpoint huts in one small district of Warsaw over the period of a year was not intended for the Nazis.

It started with food.

"Here! Quickly! Take this and keep it safe," Sendler whispered to a group of women in a dark room of the camp.

"God bless you, Irena," said the one older lady who carefully took the bag filled with bread, fruit, and some vegetables and hid it in her loose and threadbare outfit, which was marked with the infamous yellow Star of David badge.

"I will be back again in a couple of days. But next time, we need to talk about the children. I have a plan to get them out of this hell," Irena responded.

And with a little food, came a little hope; and with a little hope, came a lot of help.

After the invasion in October 1939, the PPS worked tirelessly at falsifying documents and stashing food, clean water, and medication for the Jews in the community who couldn't leave their homes. Sometimes Sendler needed to find safer homes with friends for Jewish families to hide.

Entrapment

In November of 1940, Nazis began to round up Jews and sympathizers. Around 113,000 gentile (non-Jewish) Poles were ordered to evacuate their homes and resettle in the "Aryan side" of the district so that nearly 140,000 Jews could take their place from all other districts in Warsaw. From then until April 1941, nearly 500,000 Jews were removed from their homes in Poland and Germany and sent into this segregated camp, which became known as the Warsaw Ghetto. Eighty-five thousand of the inhabitants were children up to the age of 14 (Imperial War Museums, n.d.).

Considered the biggest ghetto ever constructed in occupied Europe (one square mile), it was designed to be smaller than the population it needed to hold. It was constructed poorly on purpose and also chronically undersupplied so that the people crammed in never had a moment of peace, but instead only felt crowded, hungry, cold, and in pain.

As a social worker working for the Social Welfare Department, Sendler and her colleagues (AKA her accomplices) were requested to enter the ghetto to assess the outbreak of typhus, which was still rampant in northern Europe among the poorer communities. And within the Warsaw Ghetto specifically, it was spreading fast.

The Nazis feared it would spread beyond the boundaries of the camp, which is why they sent in the welfare sector to inspect sanitary conditions. Sendler, seeing the opportunity arise, quickly took action. She asked her friend in the Contagious Disease Department to give her the necessary papers for entry to the ghetto. In Nazi-occupied areas, it was all about securing the right papers.

Being much more than government inspectors, Sendler and her team were going to bring much more than their clipboards, pens, rubber gloves, and disease and sanitation equipment along with them. In their deceivingly small bags, they managed to stash food, medication, warm clothing, toiletries, and most importantly, false identity papers.

Over the course of the multiple visits, the women were never caught by the Nazi guards, who checked their bags upon entry and exit. Most Nazi men were far less suspect of women being involved in clandestine operations than of their male counterparts. With a little smile and some flirting to divert the soldiers' attention from their illegal possessions, the women got away with it.

But helping like this simply wasn't enough... What about the children? Sendler acted quickly and quietly.

Thanks to her official station at the Welfare Department and the Germans' absolute hatred for disease, Sendler was able to make certain strategic "census adjustments" to the ghetto list. "Testimonies submitted after the war by Sendler and her colleagues speak about a dozen or so infants taken out of the Warsaw Ghetto between 1940 and 1942" (Dzięciołowska, 2018).

Hidey Holes

Once Sendler saw the emaciated orphans walking around the ghetto, lost and alone, she sprang into action. Orphans were the first on her list to extract from the ghetto and then she cautiously began approaching parents whose children clung to their clothing. She requested the impossible of them.

"May I take your children away from you? As soon as this awful war is over, they will be restored to you, their family, and their Jewish names will be returned to them."

The Jewish mothers wept bitterly, but Sendler's plan seemed to be the only way they could possibly keep their children fed and alive. But still, people were torn. Was it safer if the family stuck together in the ghetto? Or did separating give their children a better chance to survive—even if it meant they might not ever see them again?

Irena's heart broke for them every time she saw that look of desperation in the mother and father's eyes when she asked, yet she also saw hope and gratitude. She knew these were tears of agonizing grief mixed with those of hope and relief. In time, these children became known as "the hidden children."

It's the hardest sadness to watch, she thought. This sadness was fear mixed with desperation, mixed with both hope and resignation—what an impossible choice for a parent to make.

Sendler kept the real identities and locations of the children being smuggled written on small pieces of tissue paper that she tucked into two glass bottles (later incorrectly referred to as being a singular jar). On each paper, she wrote their false names, their Jewish names, and their new current address. This was very dangerous because if the Gestapo got their hands on the bottles, they could hunt down every single one of the children, as well as the people fostering them. She needed to keep their records safe because it was immensely important to her that they find their families and regain their culture after the war.

In the following year, 1941, the Nazis tightened down the ghetto even further. A new Nazi law condemned to death any Jew found leaving the ghetto; and if any local Pole attempted to help a Jew leave, they too could expect to be executed.

Sendler and the rest of the women and men of the resistance were concerned, but took it in stride. Until this point, they had been dancing with death daily. Would a new rule intimidate them into submission? No, they must simply carry on and continue to find the right funding!

Funding came from Jewish families themselves, or Jewish communities donating together, but when that didn't cover expenses, Sendler and her underground operators pulled money from their own pockets in order to get children out. Children as young as infants and as old as teenagers were smuggled out of the ghetto, with the right papers, and became part of the wartime phenomenon of "hidden children"—Jewish children, separated from their parents, who were hidden in safe houses throughout occupied Europe, often in very small, confined spaces.

Sendler and the team would commonly use two different routes to smuggle the older children. One was through a Catholic church and the other via a dilapidated courthouse. Both buildings bordered the ghetto fence, where rescuers conducted silent digging, brick removal, and fence-cutting to make the rescues possible.

When the children were smuggled through holes in the wall into the church, nuns changed their clothes, gave them new identities, and quickly taught them all the most basic Catholic prayers. "Irena and her helpers trained the children well – they were never caught coming out of the church with Jewish children" (Kroll, 2009), but instead 'fresh' Polish Catholic children.

If children were not cloistered in a Catholic or Christian church, then they were secretly hidden all over Warsaw in the houses of Sendler's friends. Sendler had managed to organize a total of 20 "centers" around Warsaw that could take in these children.

The younger children, primarily infants and toddlers, needed to be rescued in a more elaborate manner. By carefully placing them into covered boxes with false bottoms, they could fool the guards as long as the children remained quiet. Rescuers used toolboxes, vegetable carts, gunny sacks, and a coffin once, to save these young, innocent lives from the brutality to come.

And to hide the inevitable cries of a hidden infant in her baggy clothes, Sendler used a dog. As soon as the baby would begin to whimper, she would smack the dog, which would start barking and cause the Nazis' dogs to bark in turn. The canine raucous was enough for the Nazi guards to allow the irritating women with the yapping dog to go by quickly.

Sometimes Sendler would urge the Nazi soldiers to allow her to take seriously ill children to the hospital in an ambulance. She requested permission, but then also secretly acquired a few more healthy children to hide in the back of the ambulance.

Sendler had secret names, like Klara or Jublanca, which were used when they organized liaisons, clandestine meetings, looked for new houses for the children, or issued false documents. There was a secret life within the ghetto, and she was at the center of it. Over those initial years, she and her compatriots forged and falsified a total of 3,000 documents.

As the war waged on, Sendler became more desperate and took more risks. Many times she pretended to be a Jew by wearing the yellow star and openly talking to all the others in a show of sensible solidarity. She was there because she needed to plead with more parents to allow her to smuggle their children out, as well as to see her friends. One of those very close friends was Adam Celnikier, who is presumed to have been her lover before and throughout those years in the Warsaw Ghetto.

But in July of 1942, the Nazi leadership of the Warsaw Ghetto began a campaign with the codename "The Great Action" (*Grossaktion Warsaw*) whereby they began to transport Jews to camps. A train, known as a pendulum train or Holocaust train, would carry up to 7,000 Jewish people at once 50 miles northeast to a camp called Treblinka. There, they would be separated, woman, man, and child, each to work or die alone in the newly built gas chambers.

Throughout the evacuation of the ghetto, Sendler lost many friends and was not able to save all the children, but with the help of the underground Polish resistance force, *Żegota*, she managed to get the funding to retrieve hundreds more babies and toddlers before the ghetto was completely emptied. According to Dzięciołowska (2018):

Zegota documents show that in the initial period of their activities – the beginning of 1943 – the Council ensured financial care of ninety-nine children. In May 1944, the Children's Department, with Irena Sendler as its leader, supported three hundred children in hiding.

By April of 1943, the remaining Jews in the ghetto had had enough. They continued to lose their friends and family, neighbors and lovers, who were shipped away never to be seen again. Desperate times called for desperate actions, and they began uniting under the Jewish Combat Organization (ŻOB) and the Jewish Military Union (ŻZW) within the ghetto. The rebels managed to capture one of the camp's highest SS commanders as leverage, and for that, the Nazis burnt down the whole camp.

The Warsaw Ghetto Uprising was one of the largest revolts of Jews against Nazi terror in WWII. The revolt did not end well, as most of those who stepped forward to fight died, and those who hid were captured or sentenced to death. It was heart-breaking that these men and women's last attempt to assert their self-respect was met with tragedy, yet it shows us their grit and perseverance as they fought for their humanity, culture, religion, and most importantly, their children's future.

After the revolt, the German leadership needed to respond forcefully, and so they did. Interrogations, tortures, and bribes from SS officers finally brought forth a name: Irena Sendler.

Quick Thinking

Remember the bottles filled with children's names? They were hidden in Sendler's home, each holding identical lists, most likely as insurance.

On a cold October afternoon in 1943, Sendler was at home with her friend Janina Grabowska, completely unaware of what was about to happen.

Janina was quietly reading the newspaper at the dining room table while Irena made another cup of tea. The radio was on and the fire was crackling. All of a sudden, a noise from the street caused the two of them to jump up, startled. They dropped what they were doing and ran for the windows, peering out between the curtains to the street below.

No! It can't be Irena thought, her heart pounding in her head. *The Gestapo! They are here!*

"Run!" Janina desperately whispered to Irena, who looked utterly terrified.

"But the bottles, Janina! What of the bottles?" responded Irena, as she retrieved the precious items from where they were hidden and looked desperately around. She knew the officers were climbing those stairs fast. The fire was blazing, and for a minute Irena thought to throw them in, *anything* instead of letting them be found. But Janina saw the desperation in her friend's eyes and knew how important it was to her that these names stay safe. She grabbed the bottles from

Irena and hid them under her loose clothing just as the invasive pounding on the door echoed through the apartment.

"Gestapo! Open up. Now!" exclaimed a German officer.

Once the women unlocked the door, absolute pandemonium erupted in the small flat. The Gestapo officers already knew what they were looking for and they knew who was responsible. They dragged Sendler out of the apartment and ransacked the whole place looking for the evidence they needed. Yet, they didn't find it. Janina Grabowska was very good at hiding things by now and she ensured the officers never found the precious lists while they emptied closets and broke china.

As Sendler was rushed off to a detention cell for questioning, Grabowska knew what she was to do. She returned home, retrieved a small spade, went out into her back garden, and began digging under her favorite apple tree. There, in a deep hole in the ground, she placed the bottles, then filled the hidey-hole with dirt and walked away, tears in her eyes.

The Gestapo officers had been questioning (and beating) Sendler for days and were not soft on her because she was a woman. Through the fog of torture and endless questioning, she remembers the sound of the baton repeatedly hitting her feet and legs—both feet were swollen, and her legs too.

Well, I'm not running anywhere anytime soon, Sendler thought to herself as she lay in her cell, battered and bleeding. *Both my feet are shattered.*

But the Nazi's attempts proved futile. Sendler would never give away the names of her friends or the children she had saved. She would rather die, which she was sure was the next course of action. The Gestapo, having realized that exact point, threw her in the large Warsaw prison, Pawiak, where she awaited the call for her execution.

In November, Razovsky was escorted to a new location for the fateful discipline awaiting her. She thought it was her last day on earth, grateful that the time she had was used wisely. Little did she know that she was not forgotten. Her friend at the Welfare Department, Maria Palester, had begged the Żegota chief, Julian Grobelny, to send funds to bribe the German officers to release her. At the 11th hour, she was released and sent back home.

After that, Sendler herself experienced what it was like to be rescued and to go into hiding. Not only was she traumatized, but she understood that she was at constant risk of being rearrested. She used the identity Klara Dąbrowska, a nurse working at the local hospital, for a year or so, while keeping her managerial duties at Żegota.

Thanks to her tireless work, Sendler saved 2,500 children from death.

The Close

"The Soviets are here! The Soviets are here!" screamed one of the nurses while walking past Sendler's ward.

The USSR had been in cahoots with the Nazi government at the beginning of the war, as they jointly invaded Poland, but after 1941, when the Nazis stabbed the Soviets in the back unexpectedly, allegiances quickly changed.

Hence by January of 1945, the Soviet Union had begun displacing Nazi troops across the eastern front of Poland—not necessarily with the intention of freeing the Polish people, but to take the land promised to them by the fascist regime before they were betrayed.

A new communist government was going to take hold, meaning even if the war was over for the rest of the world, Poland's new war was just beginning.

For Sendler and her team, the only thing that mattered at that point was finding all the children who were on the list and painstakingly reuniting them with their parents.

As the months turned into years, however, Sendler realized that reunification was never going to be the happy ending she had hoped for. Yes, the children were alive, but the majority of the families were forever broken, as most of the adults had perished or had been exterminated in Treblinka.

Over the remaining years of her life, Sendler never ceased her involvement in high-level state positions in politics and welfare. She joined the Warsaw City Council, the Polish Communist Workers Party, the Commission for Widows and Orphans, and the Health Commission, just to name a few. She also held an important matriarchal role in her community.

Sendler divorced in 1947 and married her longtime Jewish friend and compatriot, Adam Celnikier, who managed to survive the ghetto liquidation. He had changed his name to Stefan Zgrzembski. Together they bore three children; one sadly died in infancy. Her two children never found out they were born to a Jewish father, and when Janina did find out in adulthood, she commented that it didn't change anything, as their mother had brought them up to believe that origin and race were trivial.

When Zgrzembski passed away in 1961, Sendler found comfort once again in her first husband, Mieczysław, whom she remarried, and then divorced 10 years later. She was nothing if not a woman with her own mind!

In 1956, Sendler attempted to move to Israel with her two children, who were both Jewish and not safe in oppressive Poland, but her friends and family persuaded her to stay in Poland, expressing the sentiment "better the devil you know."

Between 1956 and 1965, Irena Sendler would be gloriously thanked for her contributions. Among her decorations were two Gold Crosses of Merit and the

Knight's Cross. She was recognized at the Yad Vashem as Righteous Among the Nations when she traveled to Israel to receive the award followed by a second visit to plant a tree in her name.

In 1967, when Sendler was 57 years old, she was diagnosed with severe anxiety and a chronic heart condition, although she kept working as a teacher at a local high school until her retirement in 1983, never for one moment slowing down.

Even as she and her compatriots were recognized in Poland, the rest of the world was completely unaware of all that Sendler and the Zegota underground had done. Not until 1999, when three American students were captivated by Sendler's story and wrote one of their own, did Sendler's name achieve the worldwide recognition it deserved. Sadly, that same year, her youngest child Adam died of a heart attack, leaving her with her eldest, whom she had named Janina after her dear friend.

The story written by the students from a rural community in Kansas, called *Life in a Jar,* was a play that depicted her life. Its popularity spread beyond the state of Kansas to be performed throughout the US. As the play gained visibility, the students continued their research and discovered Sendler was still alive. Three girls flew to Poland in 2001 to visit the 80-year-old in her home and hear more about her story. Through their visit and interview, the girls were also able to connect with the children (now adults) who were rescued by Sendler and incorporate their personal stories with those of their rescuer, making it a brilliant exhibit of her courageous life.

Many of the children Sendler saved came forward during her lifetime, and some even after her death. They were looking for the woman they called Klara, who they vaguely remember holding their hands as they were smuggled out of the ghetto. Others were merely babies in her arms, helpless and cold. Many already knew her, as she had visited them after the war. The names of Lea Balint, Piotr Zysman, Elzbieta Ficowska, and Renata Skotnivka-Zajdman were just some of the 2,500 that were never lost thanks to Irena, and later Janina. The names in those bottles were never released publicly and probably never will be for reasons of privacy and ethics.

From then on, the project became global, and an organization called Life in a Jar: The Irena Sendler Project was founded to both support Jewish communities and teach the world about the true valor of women in WWII. The student's play was then made into a book written by Jack Mayer, and then a 2009 movie called *The Courageous Heart of Irena Sendler.*

Many more awards, medals, and honors would be bestowed upon the frail yet lively Sendler in the years before her death, in 2008, at the age of 98; some awards were even given posthumously.

Irena Sendler was a woman who knew how to do what needed to be done and did it—regardless of the subtle and overt social pressure men exerted over women to keep them in their places. Her mission to save women and children was her life, and when the war ended, she just kept saving and procuring, as poverty and sadness lingered in Poland.

After all these years of interviews, articles, and books, Irena Sendler's life is now widely acclaimed, but had she not been catapulted into the public eye by the Kansas High School project, her achievements might have fallen into obscurity. A common theme throughout my series, *Brave Women Who Changed the Course of WWII,* is how women accomplished miraculous feats, yet downplayed their achievements and denied any claim to heroism. As Irena once openly stated: "Heroes do extraordinary things. What I did was not an extraordinary thing. I was normal" (World Jewish Congress, 2018).

Chapter 4:

Ebba Lund:
Red Riding Hood

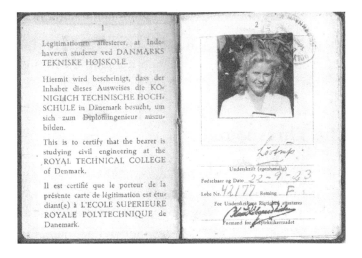

Figure 7. Identification card for Ebba Lund from the Polytechnic Institute. Image source: Frihedsmuseet 07B-13908-4, The Museum of Danish Resistance 1940-1945.

Ebba Lund was a reflection of the people of Denmark. When she spoke, she smiled—even when the adversity she spoke of was hard to hear, her eyes held the empathy and calm poise of an entire nation.

This is the story of a woman's moral fortitude and resistance from within an occupied European country—a woman who showed her community, her country, and her world just what she was made of.

While in her own way she fought against conservative ideals toward women, her inner strength shone through in the great care she demonstrated for every human being equally. She fundamentally respected other people's lives and freedoms.

Let us dive deep into the life and history of this incredibly confident individual and her journey through the unknown.

The Threshold

Ebba Kierkegaard Lund was born in 1923 in the capital city of Copenhagen, Denmark to mother, Anna Petrea Lindberg, and father, Søren Aabye Kierkegaard. Lund's father was an engineer and provided well for their family, including Ebba's younger sister Ulla. They all lived happily in their middle-class conservative life. Since childhood, Lund was an intelligent, vibrant young girl who cherished education and the pursuit of knowledge and humanitarianism.

Denmark had been relatively prosperous after WWI; its economy thrived due to fishing and agriculture, and it was an important exporter to Great Britain and Europe. Denmark's relationship with its southern neighbor, Germany, in the pre-war years was consistent and uneventful. Their shared border in South Jutland meant that a small population of Germans technically lived in Denmark and vice versa. Thus, this relationship was initially an amicable one marked by relative understanding and cooperation.

But in the late 1930s, the Danes began seeing a new face of their neighbor and they were not sure they agreed with it. Germany saw Denmark as their "Aryan compatriots" due to the Danes' fair features (blonde hair and blue eyes) and conservative mannerisms, but the Danes refused many of the German's fascist notions.

When the war began in 1939 with the invasion of the Netherlands and France, Denmark initially stood as a neutral country after signing the non-aggression pact, but that was not to last long.

Danish Resistance

The occupation of Denmark in April of 1940 is something of an oddity. The invasion was relatively soft, meaning there were few casualties and deleterious economic impacts. Thanks to the flat landscape across Denmark, the German tanks and trucks were able to traverse the land quickly and efficiently; thus, the German army entered Denmark's southern border with ease. Denmark was occupied.

Germany had no real hatred for Denmark, nor for any of the Nordic countries for that matter, because they planned eventually to unite the nations under one "Nordic Union" by the end of the war. However, for Hitler's army to access the true gem of the north, Norway, it was required to start with Denmark first. The army would have to pass through, take control of their ports, and move upwards into Norway, where they would be able to use that geographical positioning to their tactical advantage and invade Great Britain.

The Nazis knew that Denmark had more than enough food to supply their nation and that the German invasion would cut off the critical produce supply to Great Britain and the rest of the Allied nations. The Nazi regime consequently claimed that by occupying Denmark on a *de facto protectorate* agenda (exercising protective control over another country's sovereign state), it could help Denmark combat "the inevitable British invasion."

Danish Prime Minister Thorvald Stauning addressed the country during the invasion, expressing extreme unhappiness with the current turn of events, and there was some Danish military resistance at first, but soon the Danish government saw the overwhelming consequences of resisting Germany for any length of time. They were outnumbered and outsmarted by German engineering and tactical efficiency. For this reason, King Christian X of Denmark and his government permitted Nazi control of Danish foreign policy and exports in exchange for retaining political independence in domestic matters.

Two points left the Danes somewhat hopeful during this time. First, Germany's invasion of Denmark was rather subtle, and second, Denmark was home to few Jewish communities. Collectively, this meant that Germany had no intention of destroying its northern neighbor. Instead, the Nazis allowed the Danes to maintain control of their internal affairs, and throughout those initial two years, did not bother Jews living in Denmark.

Watching events unfold from her school, Lund and her friends already knew that it was wrong and senseless, but she had few tools to change anything, so she continued doing the only thing she could: Helping to publish the truth. She not only committed her days to studying, but also to working as a writer and publisher. She assisted in publishing *Frit Danmark,* or *Free Denmark,* which was a popular underground (and very illegal) newspaper that contained clandestine news for Danish resistance members and detailed unconstitutional political crimes.

In an interview Lund gave in 1994 as part of the United States Holocaust Memorial Museum, she goes on to describe how Denmark was surprised by Germany's eventual occupation in the pre-WWII years (USHMM, 1994):

> There were rumors at first, and it was not believed because they [the Danish government] said [the Germans] haven't done anything so far, why should they start all of a sudden now?

And then it became very obvious they would do something.

King Christian X resisted Nazi talk about condemning Danish Jews in turn for more control over their nation, saying (Jackson, 2019):

> The Jews are a part of the Danish nation. We have no Jewish problem in our country because we never had an inferiority complex in relation to the Jews. If the Jews are forced to wear the yellow Star, I and my whole family shall wear it as a badge of honor.

Because the king was adamant that Jews posed no concern to Danes whatsoever, the badge was never introduced in Denmark, and the King became a major symbol of freedom and strength to all Danes. Christian X was often seen prancing down the main street of Copenhagen on his horse without guards and showing moral strength in his dealings with the Germans. The children would run after him and he would be an idol of silent protest in the face of occupying Gestapo officers.

The Danish Freedom Council also spoke up during these strange years saying (*Quotes: Danish rescue and relief,* n.d.):

> We Danes know that the whole population stands behind resistance to the German oppressors. The Council calls on the Danish population to help in every way possible those

Jewish fellow citizens who have not yet succeeded in escaping abroad. Every Dane who renders help to the Germans in the persecution of human beings is a traitor and will be punished as such when Germany is defeated.

This was a bold statement that flew directly in the face of the Third Reich. News of Danish resistance to the Nazi regime was spreading, and by 1942, the country was gearing up for the inevitable.

The Move

During those two and a half years under the "Nazi protectorate," the Danes were not subject to the same rules as the other occupied nations, such as France and Belgium, where the Nazis systematically persecuted and eradicated Jewish communities and sympathizers.

Because Denmark was Hitler's "model protectorate," he allowed initial freedoms to Danish politicians as long as his regime was given control over what it wanted.

The two nations embarked on many talks, and Denmark refused many of the concessions that the Third Reich tried to impose on its people. Denmark would not give up their Jewish communities, they would not introduce the death penalty, they would not yield jurisdiction to German military courts, and they would definitely not allow their troops to be part of the German military.

In 1942, the proud and stubborn German leader remained hopeful that the Danish government would accept totalitarian rule until a rather laughable incident occurred in October of that year. It was the Danish King's birthday, and in an attempt to flatter and promote unity between the countries, Hitler chose to transmit a long-winded and rather obnoxious telegram complimenting the king on the day and his success as sovereign.

A few days later, to Hitler's horror, the King's only response was: "Giving my best thanks. King Christian." Infuriated by the slight, Hitler proceeded to throw a tantrum and completely remove Germany from occupying Denmark. He recalled his embassy staff from Copenhagen and removed the Danish ambassador from Germany. He altered the political influence on Danish control and forced their troops out of Jutland (South Denmark), sending them further north. This perceived slight initiated even more furious militant action by Hitler in the following years.

Thanks to intensive talks between the King and the Prime Minister of Denmark, honorable and lifesaving choices were made rejecting all that Germany stood for. In her book, *A Conspiracy of Decency: The Rescue of The Danish Jews During World War II*, author Emmy Werner demonstrates the contempt the Danes had for their German invaders by their sheer will to maneuver around them during the three years under protectorate rule. She writes (Werner, 2004):

The Danish bishops issued a letter of support for their Jewish community that was read in all Lutheran churches, and universities in Copenhagen and Aarhus closed down in protest. By the time the round-up of the Jews began on October 1 [1943], the Danes had succeeded in hiding almost their entire Jewish population and in moving them to coastal ports for their escape to Sweden. (p. 2)

The bishops would read at almost every pulpit in the nation (*Denmark: a nation takes action*, 2017):

Wherever Jews are persecuted because of their religion or race it is the duty of the Christian Church to protest against such persecution because it is in conflict with the sense of justice inherent in the Danish people and inseparable from our Danish Christian culture through the centuries. True to this spirit and according to the text of the Act of the Constitution all Danish citizens enjoy equal rights and responsibilities before the Law and full religious freedom.

And they took every opportunity to advocate for religious freedom as a basic human right (*Denmark: a nation takes action*, 2017):

We understand religious freedom as the right to exercise our worship of God as our vocation and conscience bid us and in such a manner that race and religion per se can never justify that a person be deprived of his rights, freedom, or property. Our different religious views notwithstanding, we shall fight for the cause that our Jewish brothers and sisters may preserve the same freedom which we ourselves evaluate more highly than life itself.

The Silent Signal

Ebba Lund was a beautiful woman, typically Danish in her looks and mannerisms with soft, elegant, and kind features and a discreet character that most likely helped her to evade German retaliation.

The 20-year-old was not only pleasant to look at, but incredibly intelligent and determined. Her quiet confidence and inner strength consistently shone through her character and actions.

In 1942, Lund completed her schooling at the Ingrid Jespersens Gymnasieskole and soon after started working for the Holger Danske resistance group based in Copenhagen. German policy had started creeping into Denmark, and civil irritation was brewing so Holger Danske existed to sabotage the Nazis in any way they could.

Following news that the Germans would be taking military action against their Jewish population in a matter of months, the resistance group began devising elaborate plans to get them out of the country.

Lund's main objective was to organize and manage the rescue of Danish Jews to neutral Sweden using the fishing boats that traveled from the northern port in Copenhagen to the Swedish coast.

Lund was called the "Girl with the Red Cap" or the "Red Riding Hood," because she wore a bright red hat (a beret) when assisting the Jews. She wasn't initially aware of the nickname, but she soon discovered that when she wore the hat in public places, people would come to talk to her and ask for help.

Lund would don the hat from then on as a silent signal to those waiting in the port; they would follow her to the appointed fisherman's boat and board in silence. She handled the funds on their clandestine trips to Sweden by paying the fishermen half before they embarked, and the other half when the fisherman reported the operation had been completed and the people were safe.

Each boat could take an average of 30 people per trip, all huddled and squashed below deck. Over the course of a month, the Holger Danske was able to help smuggle over 700 Jews out of Denmark, Lund taking part in 500 of these cases.

Facilitating the logistics of transporting Jewish families from their homes to safe houses and then on a ship to Sweden was no easy task. It took time, planning, and ample funding.

The fishermen demanded roughly 2,000 Kroner per person (roughly 200 USD in the early 1940s) to transport them across the Baltic. The high fees were meant as an insurance policy to cover the cost of their boats should the Nazis discover them smuggling Jews and cease their property (and their means to earn income).

To cover costs, Lund and the rest of the resistance had to pay out of their own pockets or ask for donations from local landowners and sympathetic businesses. Many people were willing to help, and communities got together to organize support. Reverends, fishmongers, teachers, housewives, and doctors each did their bit to hide and transport the precious cargo to safety.

Looking the Other Way

Lund ran her smuggling operations chiefly during the daytime in order to draw the least amount of suspicion. It all started in the quieter north harbor, but as the operation grew and more citizens began bringing their Jewish friends and family to the port, the more discretion the smugglers needed to exercise. In response, the Holger Danske began operating from the south harbor in addition to the north.

The citizens were not always careful in their attempts to hide the fact that they were transporting a car full of terrified Jewish refugees and often made silly mistakes. Consequently, Lund would reprimand the locals for their lack of discretion and try to teach them to be quieter and more careful. There was a learning curve for everyone participating; unfortunately, there wasn't very much room for error.

***

Ebba Lund stood very still as she watched the German soldiers walk into the harbor. Quietly they arrived in the middle of the day, just when the smuggling action was at its pinnacle.

Please, please, please don't do it, she thought to herself in a silent plea as the German officer looked directly at her across the loading dock. The sun was shining, there were crates piled high with supplies, fisherman unloading their catch from the morning, and seagulls squawking in the air. Nothing looked particularly ominous, yet the harbor fell eerily quiet as they all waited in bated breath.

The officer and his small troop looked around a little longer, quietly chatting to one another, always returning his gaze to Lund.

He knows we are hiding the Jews in the boats, so why isn't he doing something about it?, she asked herself.

The officer in charge looked at Lund one last time before turning on his heels and heading out of the port, just as quietly as he arrived.

Ebba Lund never found out why the Nazis didn't react or report the transgression, but the fact of the matter is that some German soldiers felt a certain sympathy toward the Danes, and if not sympathy, then they were swayed by a good deal of bribery.

Germans still hoped the two countries would collaborate and possibly ally themselves in later pursuits. Therefore, "the Germans were pro-Danish in a way that you couldn't believe!" (USHMM, 1994), Lund said in a filmed interview raising her eyebrows in emphasis.

She explained how Danish fishermen often chatted with members of the German Navy, which consequently gave the fishermen information to create a route to smuggle the Jews without resistance. The fishermen were clearly informed what time of day the navy patrolled the Baltic sea between Denmark and Sweden and when they would be performing repairs on their docked ships, giving time for the fishermen to usher Jews and sympathizers away.

Denmark showed a uniquely empathetic and protective approach to the so-called Jewish problem and was also given much more leeway than other occupied territories. Perhaps the Nazis were simply too naive in thinking their common "Aryan look and demeanor" would unite them. Perhaps Denmark held so much geographic and political potential for Germany that it was best not to damage the relationship. Or perhaps the Nazis were able to overlook "Danish transgressions" because Denmark had a relatively small number of Jewish citizens, so in comparison to Poland, for example, it wasn't all that important if "a few got away."

By 1943, however, the German government had militarily taken over Denmark, initiating the horror by first and foremost removing the Jews. "Rather than yield to German demands to prosecute suspected saboteurs in German military courts the Danish government resigned on August 28, 1943" (USHMM, n.d.). The German General Hermann von Hanneken would then enact martial law over Denmark.

But by the time it came for von Hanneken to ship the Danish Jews off to camps in Poland and Germany, most were already safe in Sweden. That was a rousing success for Lund, the Holger Danske, and all Danes who took part in saving their fellow citizens.

When asked, Lund mentioned that it was not possible to give an exact figure of how many people she managed to save in total. She didn't keep records, she didn't take names; she simply acted as the middleman. Others tried their best to provide estimates for her (Lund, 2014):

> As a member of the resistance group Holger Danske, she efficiently and with great courage organized a dozen fishing boats, that brought a total of between 500 and 800 people, mainly Jews, but also resistance fighters and deserters, to safety in Sweden.

Holger Danske carried on with operations trying as best they could to operate under martial law. Lund, however, was unable to continue.

The Close

It was 1943 and she had done some remarkable work in the underground organization, but she could no longer be a part of it due to her sudden illness.

Her mother and father immediately called the doctor, who visited and suggested she go to Copenhagen hospital for more tests. Lund was diagnosed with a form of blood poisoning that required her to be hospitalized for a long period. During that time, many of her colleagues and friends in the Holger Danske were captured and the resistance was dismantled by Nazi soldiers. Lund's illness struck at a somewhat opportune time; she evaded severe punishment for saving Danish Jews throughout WWII.

By the end of the war, there were over 6,000 Danish people in concentration camps around Buchenwald and Neuengamme. These were not all Danish Jews; over 2,000 were Danish policemen and some resistance fighters. The Nazis deported a total of 580 Danish Jews to the Terezin camp in Czechoslovakia, with very few sent to their deaths. Most of the Danes who were captured were returned to Denmark, and those smuggled to Sweden also returned, which meant the Danish death toll in WWII was thankfully very low in comparison to other European countries.

"The people of Denmark managed to save almost their country's entire Jewish population from extinction in a spontaneous act of humanity — one of the most compelling stories of moral courage in the history of World War II" (Werner, 2004).

In 1944, Lund married Professor Soren Lovtrup, who was a Danish embryologist and historian. They had their first child a year later, Vita, then followed by Susanne and Anders.

While being a mother and wife, Lund never stopped studying and following her passion for education and the sciences. After the war, she attended classes in immunology and chemical engineering, then attended the Technical University of Denmark for Chemical Engineering. By 1947, she had graduated and was ready to start her career.

She was employed first at the Ministry of Fisheries Experimental Laboratory at the Copenhagen University, then moved to the Carlsberg Foundation Biological Institute. Lovtrup was working in Gothenburg, so the family followed behind and settled in the town for some time. Lund and her husband divorced in 1959.

Over those years, Polio was becoming a problem in Denmark and Sweden, and Lund's epidemiological and associated laboratory experience drew her to lead the general diagnosis of the virus.

She wrote several dissertations on Poliovirus and Foot and Mouth disease and fought for her doctorate at the University of Copenhagen in 1963, as women then had a hard time being taken seriously enough to graduate.

A few years later, she stepped in as head of the Department of the Veterinary Virology and Immunology at the Royal Veterinary and Agricultural University—the first woman to ever take that position in the institution.

She remained a professor there until 1993, bringing prolific scientific concepts and opinions to the field of immunology. She was also invested in the zoonosis of diseases (transmission from animals to humans and vice versa) and treatment in various species.

Lund went on to work for the Danish Fur Breeders Association in 1969 to assist in recognizing and vaccinating distemper in mink puppies and developed the first effective antigen against plasmacytosis, which would become widely used in later years.

In 1978, she married the Head of the United States Environmental Protection Agency, Robert Berridge Dean.

In 1975, Ebba Lund, now Dr. Lund, was knighted by the Danish crown for her exemplary work both in the war and in medicine, and in 1984, she was appointed Knight of the First Degree. In the following year, she graciously accepted the Ebbe Muncks Award for her contribution to the resistance.

She sat on the board of the Danish Society for Pathology between 1968 and 1980, served as chairman of the Danish Society for Nature Conservation Research Committee, and became the vice president in

1980. Then between 1986 and 1991, she was chairperson of the Genetic Engineering Council as well as the Ethical Council.

Death was the only thing that could stop this woman, and in 1999, in her hometown of Copenhagen, the 76-year-old died peacefully, surrounded by her family.

Throughout her life, Ebba Lund wanted to prove that women could be as physically, mentally, and emotionally strong as men. Like men, women could be daring and careful, smart and career-focused. She demonstrated that she could earn money on her own, and not be at the mercy of a man. At a young age, she took charge and kept her self-worth about her for the rest of her life. She was indeed a special woman who valued her own achievements and pursuits before becoming a mother and starting a career. She dreamed big, and in turn, did something with those dreams that left a legacy for many to follow.

Chapter 5:

Marie Schmolka & Doreen Warriner: The Masterminds of the Move

Figure 8. Marie Schmolka in the 1930s.

Figure 9. Doreen Warriner in the 1940s.

Historians of late have begun to take a more critical approach to studying WWII and in so doing, they are discovering aspects of the war that have been overlooked and underrepresented. Imagine remaining in the theater well after the curtains have closed and the seats have emptied: A single note rings out and crescendos into a full symphony of the likes we've never before heard.

WWII is long over, and we are now left with pages in history books and remnants of songs, stories, and emotions felt by so many of our ancestors. In the great spotlight of history, we have idolized male heroes, such as Schindler and Churchill, and demonized the villains, such as Hitler and Stalin. It's high time we look beyond the spotlight and dig deeper.

In this chapter, we will address the lives and legacies of two women who, together and separately, made history just outside the main spotlight while it shone directly on their male counterparts. Marie Schmolka and her ally Doreen Warriner fought tirelessly to rescue children, political activists, and ordinary Czech citizens when Germany invaded Czechoslovakia. They organized the controversial Kindertransport rescue mission of Jewish children to Great Britain, and while their names are barely known, the man who funded it is glorified and honored to this day.

The Threshold

Let us begin with Marie, the senior of the two women, who saw the war start, but never saw it end. Marie Eisner Schmolka was born in 1893 in Prague, Czechoslovakia. She was the youngest of three sisters to mother Julie and father Hynek Eisner. Her father was a manager at a textile store, and the family lived in a poor neighborhood in the capital city in what was the Hapsburg monarchy. This monarchy comprised many lands, including parts of Austria, Hungary, Bohemia, and Moravia, to name a few, before its dismantling in 1918.

Schmolka's parents were known to be advocates for integration and assimilation as they spoke Czech at home but were also fluent in German, retaining friendships with German intellectuals and artists of the time, such as the exceptional novelist Franz Kafka and philosopher Felix Weltsch.

Judaism, Zionism (the nationalist ideal of creating a Jewish state of Palestine in the 20th century), and socialism were often discussed in those circles, which likely influenced the younger girls to some extent. Schmolka loved languages and enjoyed speaking both French and some English when she could.

Schmolka was often seen as the rough-and-tumble type of girl. She was unashamedly vocal in the defense of her beliefs and values. Her lifelong friend, Felix Weltsch, recalls how his mother used to say: "The youngest Eisner child is as active as a man" (Šmok & Hájková, 2018), which he charismatically implied remained a core characteristic of hers throughout her life.

Being the youngest of the sisters, she was the last to remain at home with her mother, as the two eldest had married and moved out. In her earlier years, Schmolka studied at the Higher Girl's High School in a district of Prague. She took a short hiatus from education (lacking either funding or time) and then at the age of 23, in 1916, she decided to enroll at the largest institute in Prague, Charles University or University of Prague.

When Schmolka turned 30, her mother passed away and she was left with a void in her life. She had been single until that point, and her focus was on her career as a manager at a local bank in Prague, which was a prominent position for a woman in that era.

Perhaps in looking to fill that void, she met and married Leopold Schmolka, a lawyer and a distant relation to the family. Also born and bred in Prague, the 53-year-old loved his younger wife, and the relationship was said to be a very happy one. Schmolka became a loving stepmother to Leopold's three adult children from his previous marriage and was well-provided for by the man who gifted her elegant cars and a luxurious lifestyle. Sadly, the five-year marriage ended suddenly when Leopold died.

***

Now, let us acquaint ourselves with Doreen Warriner, a woman who was sheltered by her birthplace but chose to involve herself in the war out of humanitarian interest.

Doreen Agnes Rosemary Julia Warriner was born in 1904 in Warwickshire, England, just as the 20th century was beginning in earnest and WWI loomed in the future.

Her mother, Henrietta Beatrice, was of Irish descent and her father, Henry Arthur Warriner, worked as a land agent for the Weston Park estate in Warwickshire. Warriner attended Malvern Girls College in her younger years before taking up philosophy, politics, and economics at the St. Hugh's College in Oxford in 1922 and receiving a First in 1926 (a first-class honor is a classification of earning a degree with outstanding marks).

Warriner jumped around over the next couple of years, initially studying at the London School of Economics and then moving to Somerville College, one of the

University of Oxford's first women's colleges. While conducting research for her thesis on land reform policies, she traveled to Czechoslovakia and Germany, learned the language, and attended parliamentary debates in hope of gaining access to their political views. She completed her Ph.D. in 1931 at the age of 27 and titled her thesis *Combines and Rationalization in Germany*. Because she was keenly aware of the value of education from a young age, she continued her pursuit of teaching others by becoming an assistant economics lecturer at the University College in London, where she worked till 1938.

Germany had already started showing signs of tumult, and the Soviet Union was gearing up for its own inclusion in the war, therefore talk of communism in England was generally frowned upon.

As such, Warriner had a strong interest in communism and was said to be a steadfast feminist and internationalist, who was closely monitored by the MI5 (British secret service) in possible connections with Soviets or Nazis. Those rumors were unfounded, but the investigation would continue until 1952.

Warriner was awarded the opportunity to visit Jamaica to finish her Rockefeller Traveling Fellowship (a broadening experience for post-graduates) in 1938 and was about to accept it when the news of war drew her interest away from the West Indies and toward central Europe.

Finding Their Way

"I think it will be a good idea for you, Marie," said a woman's voice coming from Schmolka's telephone piece. "You need this break so that you can mourn and move on with your life."

Palestine, Egypt, and Syria were on the itinerary, which Schmolka's former teacher, Gabriela Preissová, had been organizing for some time.

"You will meet Irma and learn more about the Zionist faith along the journey. Please come along."

Irma Polak was a member of the Czechoslovak Women's International Zionist Organization (WIZO) and influenced Schmolka to join the group. She also introduced Schmolka to the Hebrew communities and intellectuals in Prague, including WIZO founder Rebecca Sieff. When Schmolka returned from the trip, she was a changed person.

Between 1931 and 1933, WIZO primarily concentrated its efforts on the social welfare of Jewish refugees from Germany. The Nazi party was not only scaring away the Jewish population, but also anyone who did not believe in their political ideals. Due to propaganda and violence, many people started immigrating to safer neighboring counties, such as Czechoslovakia, in those early years.

After 1933, Schmolka's work picked up speed, and she began operating within the refugee community with all her might. She assisted the German citizens in the country and became a leader in the community. Her Zionist and Jewish faith ebbed her on the road to humanitarian agendas.

Her colleagues in WIZO, Milena Jesenská and Max Brod, assisted her in organizing documents, homes, financial support, and jobs for the refugees. "Her work was greatly aided by her lifelong engagement as a social democrat, together with her strong constitution, and networks opened doors to top-level politics and police stations alike" (Šmok & Hájková, 2018).

When Germany annexed Austria in April 1938 and thousands of Jews were expelled from the country, Schmolka decided to help those who were stranded in no man's land between Austria, Hungary, and Czechoslovakia. She began by organizing boats on the Danube river for the refugees to stay in while they planned a new escape route.

Impressive organizational talents along with a steadfast demeanor allowed Schmolka to join the Joint Distribution Committee and other aid organizations within the Jewish communities. As her name and reputation grew, she was invited to attend the infamous Évian Conference in July of 1938.

The conference was organized by US President Roosevelt (who sent a delegate from the US) and 31 other delegates from around the world. They met in Évian, France to come to a solution to the refugee crisis at hand. "By 1938, about 150,000 German Jews, one in four, had already fled the country" (USHMM, 2019a) and efforts were needed to understand how to compromise on immigration and relief.

Schmolka attended the conference under the League of Nations Commission for Refugees. After nine days of discussions, the world was still incredibly reluctant to allow refugees into their countries, as many economies were still recovering after WWI and the Great Depression. Jobs were scarce and feelings of resentment ran high towards the German Jews in particular.

Schmolka was the chief point person for anyone trying to get through the Czech border. It was said that any Jew who had escaped to Czechoslovakia before 1939 had seen Schmolka's face at least once. Marie Schmolka feared for her people, who were arriving in the thousands, knowing what was likely to come. Doreen Warriner, who was ready to return to Europe with a new mission, was also dreading what the Third Reich held in store.

The Move

The 34-year-old Warriner landed in Prague in October of 1938.

A month earlier, France, Germany, Italy, and Great Britain signed the Munich Agreement, which, in a desperate attempt to avert another world war, allowed Germany to annex a portion of Czechoslovakia. Great

Britain and Czechoslovakia were allies at this time, hence the outcry of shock and anger when Prime Minister Neville Chamberlain returned home saying: "I believe it is peace for our time" (Peace for our time, 2022). The English people weren't having it. Fifteen thousand people rose up in protest against the Munich Agreement in Trafalgar Square.

Czechoslovakia was the sacrificial lamb on the altar of peace, and it blew up in all of their faces when Germany disregarded the terms of the treaty. Years of resentment followed.

As per the new agreement, only the western borderlands of Czechoslovakia, known as the Sudetenland, were conceded to the Nazis. This region was currently filled with all the refugees from Germany who had escaped the previous year. When word got out, those 100,000 refugees started running into the interior of Czechoslovakia and overwhelming the relief efforts in what accumulated to over 200,000 refugees in total.

Lobbying for Lives

Warriner documented her account of the refugee rescue in her memoir *Winter in Prague,* which was posthumously published in 1984. In her initial pages, she described her arrival in Prague as such (Warriner, 1984):

I had no definite object. My only connection then was a vague commission from the Save the Children Fund, which had given me £150 for relief work, and a ready-written telegram to send on arrival – "Thousands starving children pouring into Prague, urgent appeal necessary". (p. 1)

Warriner's desperate need to help led her to request funding, or even clothes and food, from relatives and friends. She managed to accumulate a good sum of money, but when that soon dried up, she realized that she needed more help.

Her nephew, Henry Warriner, detailed his aunt's ideals in an interview with Radio Prague International (McEnchroe, 2019):

She knew the politicians, and the people at the British Embassy, so I think she really felt she could make a difference. I think she also felt that the Czechoslovaks had been let down by the Munich Agreement. While the majority of people in Britain at the time thought it was good because we were not going to have another world war, some, including her, thought it was a disgrace. I believe that many of the people who came to Prague felt that way too, feeling partly responsible for what had happened. (para. 13)

She decried the specific plight of the refugees in Czechoslovakia: "The problem was the large number of refugees who could neither return to the Sudetenland nor remain in Czechoslovakia" (Warriner, 1984). And she also knew that the camps they were staying in were in a terrible way, heavily militarized and undersupplied.

When Warriner was established as a representative for the British Committee for Refugees from Czechoslovakia (BCRC), she began operating out of an office on Voršilská Street in Prague with the intention of sending refugees to safety via Poland by train.

Her resources consisted of a monthly budget of £7,000 along with a small staff of women to help her. But in December of that year, she made the mistake of posting a letter to the *Daily Telegraph* saying how upset she was about British disinterest in foreign policy and their inaction with regard to giving citizenship to refugees in the Czechoslovakian crisis. The BCRC cut their funding drastically after that slap in the face, so once again she had to look for funding elsewhere.

As the situation worsened, her attention was pulled to more and more impoverished and overcrowded refugee camps around Prague that needed help. Although "she did not focus on Jews, many of the people she rescued were Jewish, and she did not focus on children, though in bringing out the families of anti-Nazis she also saved children's lives" (Grenville, 2011).

During these last months of 1938, Warriner and Schmolka would meet thanks to Schmolka's appeals to British humanitarian volunteers. They understood that their work interests coincided and that they could fight this battle from two fronts. Warriner had the right welfare connections in London and Schmolka had the right connections in Prague to retrieve lists of refugees. Together, they could implement a plan.

Schmolka and her colleague Hanna Stainer also began appealing to Jewish institutes and ambassadors in the free countries to assist in the plea for the refugees, especially the children. One of those appeals caught the attention of British stockbroker Nicholas Winton, who stepped up to help both financially and legally.

"Schmolka, whom Winton never met and never knew was involved, approved Warriner's bringing him in" (Klinger, 2021). And so he arrived in Prague a few weeks later and worked for months relentlessly connecting British society to the new plan, known as the Kindertransport (*kinder* is German for child) scheme.

The British government was not eager to accept adult refugees into the country. The belief was that jobs and safety were compromised with the influx of too many adults in the workplace and that this might break the delicate employment balance the country had just begun to remedy. To save face, Britain reluctantly chose to accept only the children, who were seen as less of a threat and easier to conform to British society.

The plan was to retrieve and transport hundreds of political refugee children from Czechoslovakia to Britain, but "it became clearer that the occupation was drawing nearer, and focus of the Kindertransports shifted from children of the political opponents to children of Czechoslovak Jews" (Šmok & Hájková, 2018). As the Nazi front drew nearer, Kindertransports operated throughout Poland, Germany, and Austria. Thanks to the fervent lobbying of Winton and Warriner, the plan was able to take effect (Šmok & Hájková, 2018):

> Schmolka and her team provided the majority of the lists of endangered children, including offspring of the German and Austrian refugees and children stranded in no man's land. In a race against time, the women rescue workers tried to get as many people abroad as possible.

By January 1939, Great Britain and France had agreed to pledge £12 million to rehome the Czechs, while Canada took 1,000 Sudetens.

Nicholas Winton had to return to London before the war broke out, but he never stopped working on organizing the papers and lodging for these refugee orphans. "In total, he saved 669 children" (Klinger, 2021), but his charges would inaccurately be known as "the Winton children" in history books, largely ignoring the efforts of Warriner and Schmolka.

Over the course of those nine months before war broke out, Schmolka, Warriner, and the rest of the team were able to transport almost 10,000 Jewish children to Britain, either by plane, train, or boat. The last trip was made in 1940.

Warriner was also able to arrange visas and much-needed transport for adult refugees out of Prague over the course of six months. Her nephew Henry commented on this in an interview (McEnchroe, 2019):

> Back then getting one [a visa] was a big problem. If you wanted to get a visa, your details would have to be sent to London by post, then the Foreign Office would have to look at them and send them back – a process which took a long time and it was done name by name. I think she was very instrumental in speeding up the system and she went to London quite often for this purpose, as well as to Poland and Germany.

With help from politician David Grenfell and the Sudetenland leader Siegfried Taub, Warriner made a list of around 250 male refugees deemed to be valuable to the country due to their anti-Nazi political agenda. Grenfell traveled to Britain with the list first and then organized permission for the men to be shipped by train to Britain.

Warriner wrote: "Grenfell said he must get them out at once. This was difficult because all international train connections were cut off; they could not travel across Germany. The back door to Poland was the only way out" (Warriner, 1984).

She must have saved hundreds if not thousands of Sudeten German Social Democrat refugees as well as

Jews and their families through her particular status at the British Embassy.

***

"They have just raided your office and taken Beatrice in for questioning!" said one of Warriner's informants over the phone.

Thank goodness she wasn't there that day in April, only a month after the Nazi takeover.

The Gestapo managed to retrieve many documents, but none of the important ones that contained names of Czech contacts. Warriner had cleverly kept those in her home. She proceeded to burn them all and pack her things.

I need to get into the British Embassy now! she thought, grabbing only what she desperately needed.

Warriner stayed in the embassy for a few weeks falsifying the last documents that allowed refugees to exit German borders, but soon enough, the embassy itself was under threat of siege, and the word was out for Warriner's arrest.

The very next day, she boarded a plane. She was not returning home, but rather continuing her Ministry of Economic Affairs duties in Cairo, Egypt.

In 1941, she received her OBE (Officer of the Most Excellent Order) for her work with the British Committee for Refugees from Czechoslovakia, and then between 1944 and 1946, she worked under the United Nations Relief and Rehabilitation Administration in Yugoslavia running the food supply.

The Close

Marie Schmolka and her co-workers at the Committee for Refugees were one of the first groups of people to be arrested in Prague by the Gestapo in March 1939, the day after the Nazi invasion.

Schmolka was locked away for two months and experienced harrowing conditions and grueling eight-hour interrogations. She was a diabetic, but she was denied insulin and this, together with a lack of food and water, caused her to become life-threateningly ill. Thanks to protests by the Protectorate ministers and the Czech Women's Movement, Schmolka was eventually released, but her health was severely compromised.

The terror was not to end there. The SS head of Jewish Emigration, Adolf Eichmann, would "headhunt" Schmolka, along with her associate Emil Kafka, and task them to travel to Paris and then to London to advocate for rapid Jewish immigration approvals.

At that stage, Nazi policy allowed mass Jewish emigration out of Germany. Shortly after, however, borders were sealed and the top-secret "Final Solution" was implemented, which decreed the extermination of the Jewish race.

When WWII officially broke at the end of 1939, Schmolka and Kafka were stuck in Britain, unable to return home. Schmolka's time in London was not a happy one, as "some of the people whom she had helped to emigrate to Britain didn't want to give her place in the refugee organization... fearing to lose their new status and jobs" (Šmok & Hájková, 2018).

She managed to continue working as a social worker in the Czechoslovak Zionist and Quaker movements. She moved in with her friend, activist and author Mary Sheepshanks, in Gospel Oak, northwest London.

Even though she helped so many arrive in England, she was shunned and marginalized when it was her turn to need a helping hand. She would often find racist graffiti scratched on the door ("filthy refugee," for example), questioning why Mary Sheepshanks was helping her.

Schmolka died from a heart attack in 1940 at the age of 46. Stubborn as always, she consistently refused medication and advice to slow down. She was said to have worked herself to death.

Among those who attended her funeral in Golders Green Jewish cemetery in London were many prominent names in Czech emigration organizations, including members of the exiled WIZO group Schmolka worked with many years. In 1944, the organization changed its name to The Marie Schmolka Society under the leadership of Nelly Engel and published a memorial booklet in her honor soon after.

***

Meanwhile, after her work in Yugoslavia, Warriner returned to London in 1947, eventually becoming a development economics professor at the University College London School of Slavonic and East European Studies, where she became interested in land reform.

In 1972, Doreen Warriner died from a stroke.

Her nephew, Henry Warriner, studied his aunt's involvement in the war through her memoirs from 1930 to her death. In 1984, the family posthumously published Doreen Warriner's accounts, titled *Winter in Prague,* and then in 2019, Henry himself authored a heartwarming book in his aunt's memory titled *Doreen Warriner's War.*

In 2020, the University College of London commemorated her with a ceremonial unveiling of a plaque in her honor. The ceremony was attended by her friends and family, fellow lecturers, as well as the daughter of Sir Nicholas Winton.

Throughout her life, Warriner was very secretive about her work due to the danger she would be in if too many stories got out, and in order to distance herself from the past so that she could move on with her life.

The same can be said of Maire Schmolka. Even though her years on earth were few, the time she did spend was active and full of life, albeit private. She was always expecting good news and remained hopeful that with a little grit and perseverance, anything was possible.

***

The true tragedy of the war, aside from the incredible loss of life, is its repercussions on refugees—the failure of the Allied governments to intervene earlier and accept greater numbers of refugees; the families who were torn apart, never to see each other again; and the fact that very few children ever reconnected with their mothers and fathers, many of whom forgot or lost their Jewish faith.

The underlying tragedy is not recognizing the women who risked life and limb and endured persecution and imprisonment to do a job that governments and civilian men didn't do. Many of us have heard of Sir Nicholas Winton—he was knighted by the Queen of England in 2003 for his humanitarian efforts during WWII. But historians and institutions so easily forgot the two women—Schmolka and Warriner—who were the operating force behind the Kindertransport movement.

"While Winton is memorialized in a statue at Prague railway station and was awarded the Czech Republic's highest state honor, there is no shrine to Schmolka" (Tait, 2019). Associate professor Anna Hájková at the British University of Warwick so eloquently mentioned: "She is one of many women erased by history," and thanks to the Marie Schmolka Society, many of these achievements are now lit up for the world to see.

Chapter 6:

Andrée de Jongh:
Brave DéDée

Figure 10. Twenty-five-year-old Andrée de Jongh. ©Imperial War Museum (HU 55451).

The final chapter ventures into occupied France and Belgium to examine the life and legacy of a brilliant young woman who led fallen Allied airmen and special operatives to safety from behind enemy lines. She risked her own life repeatedly because she refused to bow down to abusive authority and comply with dehumanizing policies.

The story of Andrée de Jongh is one of defiance. It is remarkable and inspiring, especially reflecting on her involvement in the war and its repercussions on her home country of Belgium. She carved out her own path and answered to her conscience alone. Her young independent spirit and her fierce nature transformed her into a woman who would not take the easy way out.

The Threshold

Andrée Eugénie Adrienne de Jongh was born in the flat, verdant land of Belgium during the middle of the Great War (WWI) in 1916. Belgium borders France and the Netherlands to the west and east and Luxembourg and Germany to the south and southeast. The North Sea makes up its northern border.

The de Jongh family lived in a Brussels district called Schaerbeek, and her father Frédérick, the principal at the local primary school, was held in high regard among the community.

De Jongh had an extremely close connection with her father, who would later become her greatest ally in the battle against a fascist power. Her mother, on the other hand, had been staying in a nearby town caring for de Jongh's ill little sister. For the time being, it was just Andrée and her dad, as they didn't know when her mother would return.

In her younger years, de Jongh looked up to a substantial female role model, the WWI British Red Cross nurse Edith Cavell. De Jongh's heroine died right in her birth town of Schaerbeek while trying to rescue Allied soldiers out of Belgium and into the Netherlands during WWI. De Jongh was so inspired by Cavell that she endeavored to follow in her footsteps and eventually did so by entering college to study nursing in her early 20s. She also had a penchant for art and worked as a commercial painter in the northern town of Malmedy after graduating from school.

A Lasting Impression

The front door slammed open and her father rushed into the house. His face was pale and his features a mixture of fury and fear.

"Father! What is it?" asked Andrée frantically as her father sat down heavily at the kitchen table and hid his face in his hands. He began sobbing, something Andrée had never seen before.

"Father! Please, speak to me. You are frightening me," Andrée said, placing a hand on his shoulder.

"They are here Andrée. It's happening again. The government has been taken by force by the Germans and our King has given up. How could this happen again?"

Indeed, thought de Jongh as she looked at her father in pity and reflected fear. It had taken Belgium so long to pick up the pieces since 1918, and now, they were experiencing déjà vu and the same emotional rollercoaster turned many fears into extreme anger.

How could King Leopold III surrender so easily? she wondered, dumbstruck. *It had only been 18 days!*

The year was 1940. Due to Belgium's geographical position within Europe, it was vulnerable to invasion. Both in WWI and in WWII the Germans used this weak and viable geographical location to pursue greater threats in Europe by invading France from the northeast. And so it was that Belgium was simply, "in the way" once again with Germany trampling through and terrorizing them to reach the prized France.

Although they knew it to be unlikely, Belgians couldn't help but hope that they would be left alone and the war would rage around them. When hopes were dashed by Germany's invasion, a form of national PTSD started showing in the older generation, which only brought resentment and resistance from the youth.

Because de Jongh and her friends were born during a war and their childhood had been molded around the idea of invasion and annexation, they seemed to possess an inner strength that their elders had not demonstrated. This time around, there was something vastly different about the country and its people. De Jongh was not going to lay down and hope for the best. This time, they were going to fight back.

De Jongh knew who the enemy was—the antisemitic Germans.

They dislike the world so much that they needed to wage war on it twice! she thought to herself angrily. *Preposterous. I will not stand for it.*

She understood perfectly well that antisemitism was not a belief held by the majority of Germans or Europeans and that many good Germans did not support the Nazi views. But she also understood with great clarity that this was another war, and whether she liked it or not, she needed to help, just like her hero Cavell did.

The 23-year-old Andrée was a wise soul who seemed to already know the value of human life and the power of returning dignity and breath to others. She was a beautiful young girl with vivid blue eyes who showed intelligence and kindness. Her unruly curly hair alluded to her wild and passionate character, and she was short, slim, and as you might guess, fairly unassuming.

This image she portrayed was exactly what got her through some of the scariest moments in her clandestine missions. Naivety and innocence became the shield she wore to hide her true strength from the face of men.

The Move

"We cannot just sit in here and pretend that nothing is happening out there!" Andrée said to her friend sitting at the opposite end of the table while pointing angrily at the door. "Airmen are literally falling from the sky and they have nowhere to hide. Let's guide them out of occupied territory so they can rejoin the fight against these Nazi pigs!"

It was a warm summer night in 1940 and de Jongh was tired, restless, and consumed by anger. After the invasion a month ago, people were absolutely and utterly overwhelmed.

Operation Dynamo (AKA Dunkirk) was the planned evacuation of British soldiers from the surrounding German army after the Battle of France in late July. The conflict in the Netherlands and Belgium had left many British and Belgium soldiers stranded, and the majority of these soldiers were airmen who were bombed down by German guns and taken as POWs.

Although the Allies managed to save over 198,000 British and 140,000 Belgium soldiers, some historians view the operation as a logistical failure because of the vital supplies left in France and Belgium, which the Germans happily took for themselves upon victory.

De Jongh had been working as a volunteer nurse in the local German-controlled hospital in Brussels during this time and was so appalled by the numbers of injured and dead soldiers arriving, that she couldn't just watch anymore. Many of these men were POWs, British soldiers, who once released from care, were sent to work in POW camps in Germany and Poland.

De Jongh spoke with these men and truly sympathized with their cause, so she helped them send secret letters back to their families in Britain through her connections with the Red Cross. But what if she could smuggle not just letters but the men themselves back home?

It Starts Small

German SS officers would make weekly visits to the hospital recovery wards to assess whether the POWs were ready to go to camps and work. The Nazi sentiment was that it did not matter whether the man lived or died, as long as he wasn't free.

De Jongh came up with a brilliant plan to help the soldiers stay safely on the hospital premises. She would cleverly fake the Allied soldiers' conditions by applying a vile-smelling ointment onto their bandages just as the SS officer entered the ward. As the inspectors walked past each cot with their clipboards and pen, they would scribble down the man's condition and move on. But walking past de Jongh's patients would bring the inspectors to presume the worst based on the horrid smell emanating from the men. They would quickly walk past, not thinking anything of the innocent nurse standing to the side.

De Jongh would then proceed to sneak the men out of the hospital in the dead of night and place them into safe houses around Brussels, to be smuggled away later or to wait out the war.

She did not waste any time making trustworthy friends and acquaintances who believed in freedom and peace. Over that year of watching, planning, and despising the Nazis, de Jongh decided that if she was going to fight back, she needed to know her opponent better. Therefore, she made sure to get her hands on any official material about the German POW regulations and movements to study how to maneuver around them.

The young de Jongh made the right connections with the right people—namely older compatriots in this smuggling ring, Henri de Bliqui and his cousin Arnold Deppè. The threesome initially called themselves the Triple Ds after the commonality in their last names. Baron Jacques Donny would join later as their treasurer, and together in 1941, they would come to be known as the core founders of the *Réseau Comète*, or the Comet Line.

Their mission was to escort soldiers to safety from Belgium through occupied France, through neutral Spain, and finally to British-controlled Gibraltar, where the soldiers would be firmly in British hands. This involved a vast network of people willing to hide, escort, falsify papers, and fund the trips. As with many other enormous exploits in history, the Comet Line started small and shakily.

The immense risk these people were taking would dawn on them when their friend, de Bliqui, was arrested in April 1941 and later executed. They had been working with a German mole and had been compromised. To de Jongh, this meant that they simply had to stay on the move and one step ahead of the enemy.

Thanks to the help of Deppè and his family connections in France, the Comet Line began its journey from one safe house to another down Europe and into Spain. Deppè spoke to countless people and acquaintances over that recruitment period, organizing houses and funding wherever possible.

Once a viable route had been established in July 1941, de Jongh and Deppè would make their first official journey together down the European continent with 10 Belgian soldiers and a middle-aged English woman called Miss Richards who, unbeknownst to them, was a member of the Belgian resistance. Frédérique Alice Dupuich went on to be trained by the SOE (Special Operations Executive) in England.

The group arrived in Spain after having trekked for weeks down through Belgium, France, and then through the bitter cold of the jagged Pyrenees mountain range. De Jongh and Deppè were not meant to stay long, and quite literally dropped them off in a hurry just within the border before they retreated into France.

This first trip ended in disaster. The group was immediately arrested and taken into custody for crossing the borders illegally. Although Spain was a neutral country, the Spanish dictator, General Francisco Franco, had allied himself with Nazi ideologies, so he upheld some of their policies, which prevented the Belgium refugees' flight to Britain. Three of the soldiers were killed, and the others were taken to prison camps, including the resistance spy Frédérique Alice Dupuich, who was later to escape and make her way to England.

This was a wobbly start for sure, and de Jongh certainly learned her lesson. She knew they needed to broaden their base of allies as well as guarantee British assistance through the port of Bilbao in Spain for future missions to succeed.

Two months later, de Jongh and her faithful accomplice, Deppè, would make their second trip down the line. This time, they split up, each taking different routes—Deppè with six men and de Jongh with three. De Jongh's route was much longer and harder to travel, but safer as it avoided populated areas.

Unfortunately, Deppè was betrayed by a German informer, and the group was arrested by the Gestapo before they could reach their next safe house. He was taken prisoner in August 1941 and remained at a POW camp for the rest of the war. But de Jongh was still traveling along her route, stopping at the predestined locations to rest and eat, then moving onwards either by train or foot.

When they reached the northern coastal town of Bilbao in Spain, de Jongh and her three wards entered the British Consulate exhausted and relieved. One of the three men was Scottish soldier James Cromar, credited with being the first escaper on the Comet Line.

Figure 11. Jim Cromar (Mad Cromar), Comet Line number one escaper.

"Excuse me, young lady, but who did you say you were?" asked the British official behind the desk. De Jongh had just finished explaining to him who she was and why she was there. Frustrated, she began again, "My name is Andreé de Jongh. I am from Belgium and

I have a plan to help your countrymen. Are you willing to listen or am I to be constantly dismissed?" she asked with an edge to her voice.

The older man was taken aback by her forthright attitude and smiled at her indulgently as if she were a feisty child. De Jongh quickly realized she still wasn't being taken seriously and pointed to the British officer by her side. "This is Officer Cromar, he knows better than anyone else what this escape route can do. Are you willing to help us get this operation running in a more organized manner or will I have to figure it out on my own?"

Cromar smiled wryly, feeling slightly sorry for the speechless man behind the desk.

De Jongh was decisive and she wasn't going to take no for an answer, but behind her assertiveness was desperation. The British workers at the consulate were not remotely convinced that she had indeed crossed those 500 miles and worried she was a German spy trying to infiltrate the exfiltration of Allies.

A good three weeks passed before de Jongh got her answer from the British government.

"We have decided to assist you, but what control are we to have over this operation?"

"None at all, except financial," was de Jongh's reply. She firmly believed that her work would be more successful with fewer British and Belgian government hands involved. She and her friends would find the Allied men, group them, and transport them down. The British Empire only needed to pay for it.

And pay they did, because the cost to employ guides across Europe, including housing, food, medication, and documents was not cheap. But the trained bomber pilots of the Allied armies were in short supply, which made the military desperate to get these healthy, stranded airmen back to England and into fighter planes to resume their offensive over Europe.

Betrayal Down the Line

After Depèe's arrest, De Jongh concluded that Belgium was not safe anymore. By August of 1941, de Jongh had moved the Comet Line main office from Brussels to Paris. Her father, who had been involved with the operation the whole time, decided to coordinate the rescue of British airmen from Belgium fields and forests before the German troops arrived to capture them, whereas de Jongh coordinated French evacuations and escapes from Paris.

The operations behind the Comet Line were complex. "Organizers needed to recover fallen airmen, procure civilian clothing and fake identity papers, provide medical aid for the wounded, and shelter and feed the men as they moved along their long obstacle course" (Martin, 2007).

With the help of MI9 intelligence officer Airey Neave, the operation was able to transmit the names and locations of the British soldiers to London, and from there, obtain papers for the soldiers to fly back to Britain.

The men—stranded and sometimes injured—would be lodged in a safe house in a village or a remote farm. Then they were brought to collection points in larger cities, such as Paris and Brussels, and then spirited away down the Comet Line to safety. This entailed hundreds of miles of travel and hundreds of line workers, all assisting these people to escape.

After they arrived at the foothills of the Pyrenees to a small town called San Sebastian, they were snuck into Spain. From there, the men would be picked up by British officials in Bilbao and driven down to Gibraltar. Finally, they would jump on a plane that would ferry them all back to England.

Even though the Comet Line was the largest and most important escape route out of Europe, it was not the only escape route working at the time. Some British officers who had been stranded and hadn't managed to escape in Dunkirk set up their own routes and worked together with de Jongh and her team. Ian Garrow, for example, and his Pat O'Leary Line operated out of France. Garrow would later be captured and imprisoned, which left a French woman named Mary Dissard in charge of the line.

The German soldiers, or Axis agents and collaborators (who were usually German citizens who spoke fluent English and who lived in these countries for a long time), would sometimes impersonate a British or American airman and then infiltrate their underground network.

De Jongh was fearful. Too many of her friends and acquaintances had been taken by the Gestapo, imprisoned, tortured, and killed. Then in 1943, many more were betrayed and taken into custody by one of the Comets Line's newest members, Henri Dericourt, who turned out to be a German informant.

German officials knew well what was going on in the background, or better, the underground. Their keen awareness emphasized their desire to find and stamp out whoever was helping these soldiers get back home.

As a result, new escape routes needed to be established over the course of the war to evade commonly patrolled areas, making escape line work one of the most dangerous forms of resistance work.

Although those who were working in the escape line were not soldiers or Jews, they were still given the worst sentence for their crimes of assisting foreign troops. Unlike the soldiers, who were (mostly) protected by the Second Geneva Act (preventing the killing of POWs in war), the resistance workers had no such guarantees, and if they were captured, they were either sent to concentration camps or suffered torture and execution.

But de Jongh's continued work from 1940 to 1943 would make her famous. She became known as the postmistress (or postman) because she affectionately called her evacuees "her parcels." Her introductory speech to the men at the beginning of their journey to freedom usually went like this (van der Drift, 2020):

> My name is Andrée… but I would like you to call me by my codename, which is Dédée – which means Little Mother. From here on I will be your little mother, and you will be my little children. It will be my job to get my children to Spain and freedom.

So many people, friends and foes, refused to believe that this young girl with ankle-high socks and a flowery dress was the leader of the Comet Line. They always assumed it was run by a tough man. And as one of the many airmen assisted into Spain once said in dismay: "Our lives depend on a schoolgirl!" (Corbett, 2007).

Fit In or Be Captured

The people who couriered these men to safety were often teenagers and young adults, mostly women, as they were seen as innocent and of no concern to most Nazi soldiers. The local women on the routes needed to support the soldiers through the journey and show them how to be indistinguishable from a local.

The soldiers had to feign being either French or Spanish, but as one soldier lightly remarked on the matter: "It is not an easy matter, to hide a foreigner in your midst. Especially when it happens to be a red-haired Scotsman or a gum-chewing American from the West" (Wondrium, 2020). These airmen had to disguise themselves and comport themselves in a European manner so as not to alert the German soldiers of their true nationality while they ventured south to freedom.

"What brand do you smoke?" asked the guide, a young boy no older than 15, as he hurriedly packed some food supplies in a bag.

"Lucky Strike" replied the American officer, as he pulled out a stick from his soft packet.

"No, that won't do," said the young boy taking the unlit cigarette out of his mouth and throwing it on the ground.   "They will know. Here, take these until we arrive at the border."

The young boy handed the American a fancy French brand of cigarettes.

Gauloises? Great. Just great, thought the American airman frustrated as he opened the new packet and pulled one out with his lips. *How do I even pronounce that?*

The border officials (both in France and Belgium) were so adept that they could not only spot an American from the bunch, but also sniff him out. American and British tobacco had a particular quality to the odor that was distinctively foreign—thus, the obvious need to use local brands. German soldiers were just as equipped to spot these "sly rats" as the "sly rats" were to surpass their vigil.

The fleeing soldiers were ordered not to speak a single word and to walk and behave as a typical European would. Even eating could get them in trouble as Americans tended to eat with their knife and fork in different hands. American soldiers also tended to have a different gait and mannerisms; for example, keeping their hands in their pockets, something French men never did, and chewing gum, which was not known in Europe.

In the late 1930s, America had not yet faced the extent of economic hardships and food shortages that Europe had, so when American soldiers traversed poverty-stricken Belgium, France, and Spain, they wondered why they were being fed so little and often made a fuss about it. They tended to be arrogant and brash and didn't listen to their younger French and Belgian couriers. The British soldiers, accustomed to food rationing, were more compliant. Manners aside, many managed to make it through the line to safety, but many others were also discovered and captured. The routes weren't always foolproof.

For de Jongh, the world of underground operations was in her blood. Author Derek Shuff recounts de Jongh's modus operandi in his book *Evader* about an English pilot whom de Jongh assisted in escaping Germany mid-war (2010):

A woman couldn't carry a gun or fly a bomber jet, but she could walk unnoticed, striding down a street in a wool coat and sensible shoes as if on her way to the market or a typist's job, trailed quietly by two or three wayward soldiers in disguise. (p. 15)

Throughout Belgium's four years of occupation, de Jongh was able to escort 118 people to safety through her Comet Line; 80 of them were British airmen.

A British soldier, Bob Frost, recalled fondly that when he was 19 years of age, he was rescued by de Jongh and her friends via the Comet Line. He spoke fondly of the people who helped him through: "I fell in love with them totally, absolutely. They knew the price if they were caught. It was heroism beyond anything I can tell you" (Wondrium, 2020).

The Close

Just as 1943 had begun, de Jongh was captured on her eighteenth mission to Spain.

The story goes that either she had been betrayed by a local farmer (who had seen her escorting three British airmen into a safe house) in the Pyrenees mountains of southern France *or* one of her accomplices had been brutally tortured by the Gestapo, revealing the whereabouts of all the safe houses. Who gave her up is still unknown, but we do know that her capture was sudden and unexpected. The group she was escorting all awoke the following morning to the Gestapo entering the small house and pulling them out of their beds.

So close! thought de Jongh as they dragged her away into their van.

They were only five miles away from the Spanish border and had to stop the extra night due to a key river crossing having flooded. If it had not been so rainy and wet, they might have been able to evade the raid.

The 27-year-old de Jongh was sent to Fresnes prison in the French capital for some time. There she was tortured and questioned profusely on her involvement in the Comet Line by both the Gestapo and the Abwehr (German intelligence). De Jongh was reportedly more fearful for her father and friends than for herself. She took the next years of her life in strides, even if they were to be her most torturous.

In prison, she refused to mention her true involvement or provide names of those who worked with her, but thanks to her youth and false naivety in responding to questions, she was assumed to be a small cog in the operation.

De Jongh was sent to Ravensbrück concentration camp in Germany and left for dead until their liberation in April 1945. Over the course of those two years, de Jongh became severely emaciated and was treated just like hundreds of her campmates.

She had lost so much weight that she became unrecognizable among the crowd, which turned out to be a lifesaver. In 1944, the Gestapo found out that "DéDée" was actually Andrée de Jongh, but they could not distinguish her from the other stick-thin and sluggish people within the concentration camp fence and they stopped pursuing the matter altogether.

Her father, Frédéric, had not been so lucky. He was captured (along with the majority of the organization) in 1943, imprisoned, tortured, and murdered in 1944 when they found out his true connection to DéDée.

While the Comet Line workers were being betrayed and imprisoned, the Comet Line still ran and helped over 700 more Allied airmen and soldiers to safety.

When her camp was finally liberated and de Jongh had miraculously managed to survive, she was obviously very ill, underweight, and traumatized. She returned home to her mother, who had remained uninvolved throughout the war, to heal physically and emotionally. The news that her father and friends had died was difficult to bear.

When her life returned to her "new normal", she chose to keep up with her nursing by finishing her studies and then being stationed in Northern and Central Africa, where she worked at leper hospitals in Ethiopia, the Congo, Senegal, and Cameroon.

While in Ethiopia, de Jongh was notified that her mother's longtime illness had returned and that she was going to die soon. De Jongh had no way of getting home to Brussels in time to say goodbye, but thanks to the grateful and gracious men at the Royal Air Force base nearby, she was able to make an unscheduled flight from Addis Ababa to Belgium. This was an enormous sign of respect from the pilots. She managed to say goodbye to her mother and then she immediately returned to Africa.

When she worked in Congo in 1959, she was interviewed by the novelist Graham Greene. He published *In Search of a Character: Two African Journals,* which included a chapter on her candid recollection of the events of the war and her love for nursing and Africa.

In 1946 she was awarded the British George Medal and the United States Medal of Freedom. The Belgian Army gave her the honorary rank of lieutenant-colonel and later made her Chevalier (merit) of the French Legion of Honor and also Chevalier of the Order of Leopold. Then in 1985, at the age of 69, Belgian King Baudouin awarded her the noble title of Countess.

When she was too ill to work in Africa, she and her colleague Thérèse de Wael returned to Brussels.

In late 2007, the 90-year-old de Jongh succumbed to illness in a Brussels hospital. Her funeral was held in a large cemetery where many could mourn and honor her. Her wish was to be interred in her parents' family crypt in her small hometown of Schaerbeek.

The books written, the memoirs published, and the documentaries made were wonderful renditions of the life of a woman who endured hell, but never stopped serving others. Her life is a testament to the power of a woman's mind and will in an era when women were overlooked and undermined throughout society. What we see is that de Jongh was vastly different from many of her peers. She didn't walk; she ran the extra mile to organize, plan, and preserve life. I would like to leave you with her thought: "As for those of us who helped create this brighter future, I can only add: Don't thank us, for we had the joy of fighting, without striking a blow" (Shuff, 2010).

Conclusion

Figure 12. Fight like a girl.

It is easy to picture the famous faces who were mentioned as honorable contributors to justice in all the wars that raged, but again, looking for heroes in history doesn't always mean we will find the strong, noble, and fit.

In this book, we were reminded that heroes are everyday people: The typist, the teacher, the social worker, the housewife, or the schoolgirl who were inconspicuous, shy, nervous, and who took on monumental tasks while denying any suggestion of heroism.

Like an ordinary rock buried thousands of miles within the crust of the earth, the greater the pressure and temperature exerted on it, the more it compresses and forms crystals and diamonds. So it was with our women rescuers; their immense need and pure desire to help, coupled with their willingness to take great risks during an extremely perilous time, transformed them from ordinary young women into role models and heroes.

All of the eight women whom you have come to know over the course of this book showed us the power of leadership, kindness, and strong moral convictions in a time of extreme fear, foreboding, and fragility. They started small, testing the waters and finding out what they were capable of, they pivoted when something wasn't working well, and they soon became pillars in their communities—women whom many others leaned on for the strength, courage, and determination that they struggled to find within themselves.

They risked life and limb to save others from certain pain and death so that children could be cared for and grow old, so that families might be able to stay together or reunite after the war, and so that men they didn't know could rejoin the fight and later return home to their loved ones.

While there are no damsels in distress within these pages, neither are there superheroes in capes. When your life is at risk, it is much more advantageous to be inconspicuous than to stand out, which highlights a basic principle: To be an effective rescuer in WWII, the best disguise was looking and acting ordinary.

Heroes come in all shapes, sizes, and guises, and sometimes we need to look a little harder to find them if they belong to an underrepresented group, such as women and people of color. But make no mistake, they were there fighting in World War II, they are fighting today, and they will continue doing so well into the future—regardless of whether we see their name in the news, if they win an award, or if their stories make it into the historical canon.

As we study the past, let us remember that, even if women's legacies have been lost to history, either by being inaccurately depicted or deviously withheld, there is often some evidence to be found revealing their hidden but powerful work.

And today that means something because our news in the West has become increasingly polarized. Objectivity and truth are no longer the paragons of journalism they once were, and that directly impacts how our history is recorded.

To find a recent example of the tenuous relationship between the past and the present, we need look further than Russia. In January of 2022, Russian President Vladimir Putin gave the go-ahead for his army to invade Ukraine.

Their reason? Land—but a more accurate answer might be power. Ukraine was a former Soviet Republic, and not just that, but "behind only Russia, it was the second-most-populous and -powerful of the 15 Soviet republics" (Masters, 2022). Ukraine is a huge producer of agriculture in the region, home to defense industries, and its location near the Black Sea also makes it a strategic military stronghold.

The Russian president's choice to invade a country in this day and age is almost as preposterous as it was 80 years ago. Almost eight million Ukrainians fled for their lives. Many are dying as I write this, and many more are becoming displaced.

The women we have spoken about are just a few whose hope for humanity and brave actions altered the course of the future for so many. We need to only look a little further back in time and with a little more scrutiny, to see their beautiful strong female features pasted on articles with the heading "Hero."

If Marie Schmolka had never finished her education, if Andrée de Jongh hadn't insisted on being heard and taken seriously, and if Irena Sendler had not been quick enough to hide her precious lists, where would the world be today?

It may be hard to believe that these few women could have made such an impact on the war's outcome, but one pair of hands or one sharp mind can make the biggest difference.

Many brave men fought and aided in the war efforts in various ways. Many of them were recognized, by name, for their honorable contributions during WWII and shortly thereafter—internationally and by their respective governments. That is how it should be, and far be it from anyone—male or female—to denigrate their memory or diminish their achievements.

That said, we all know that power has historically rested within the government and the military, which were overwhelmingly male-dominated (and still are, to a slightly lesser degree). These institutions are typically closed and self-perpetuating, with deep pockets and vested self-interests; moreover, it has always been beneficial to those involved, that they remain this way.

Meanwhile, women make up roughly half the population—even more during the World Wars as a hugely disproportionate number of men died on the battlefield. Women may not have typically been the breadwinners in the first half of the 20th century, but the load of work they carried prior to the war in many societies, one can argue, was much more than half. After WWI, their load increased even more as they continued to raise children and work inside and outside the home. With minor ebbs and flows over the years, that trend has continued.

Now let's look back on our heroic women in WWII. They worked diligently behind the scenes of extremely important and risky operations to save lives, yet their contributions were largely unrecognized.

Imagine if the women rescuers had been more concerned with their titles, salaries, achievements, and recognition among their peers. And what if, when they saw their male counterparts being publicly lauded, they had thrown up their hands, ceased their duties, and protested? How dare these men overshadow them? How dare they earn more money? How dare they exercise more freedom?

The rescue operation would have stood no chance of success. It was never about a single person; it was about the collective effort. They had little to no time to think about what was coming tomorrow, much less after the war. They knew the consequences of their actions and they kept going without fussing over who did what and how they got paid.

It was universally understood among the rescuers that their work was so much bigger than their personal acclaim and agenda. It was about getting the children, women, and men who huddled together in fear and uncertainty to safety—not about the final gain, the final word, or the final pat on the back. These eight women typified the 20th-century mentality of "just getting on with it" for the sake of doing the right thing, not for the glory of it.

It is great to want to delve into the work at hand, make a mark, and be the honored hero, but it is even greater to believe in your own worth and contribution when you are not in the spotlight giving a thank you speech, but rather on the sidelines, looking on, and clapping with the others.

These were ordinary women who quietly and expertly shuffled people across Europe by foot, train, or plane with such immense bravery and determination that some of their stories are almost impossible to believe.

But learn about them we must, because in doing so, we honor these unsung heroes. We recognize their names, their personalities, their contributions to the fight against fascism, and how their strength flew in the face of the typical (and even ideal woman) of the time, who was generally quiet, submissive, and relegated to the home. Not only do these women from WWII deserve our recognition and appreciation, but we also need their inspiration today to stand up for those facing injustices—whether they're our family members, neighbors, or people living halfway across the world we don't know.

WWII was a large-scale aberration, but today, women, children, religious and ethnic minorities, displaced persons, immigrants, people with disabilities, victims of hate crimes and systematic oppression all continue to endure injustices, and if we sit idly by, then what? Let's learn from our foremothers and take action.

We have spoken at length about refugees during WWII. It is estimated that between 40 and 60 million people were displaced during the war years. Today, tragically, there are still millions of refugees fleeing Ukraine, Syria, and Afghanistan, to name but a few war-torn regions of the world.

No matter where you are in the world, you can advocate for the rights of refugees and asylum seekers. Just like some of our heroes in this book, you can find out more about how to help.

There is still so much work to be done today to help refugees fleeing war and political unrest. For example, you can donate money to a specific organization, such as the UN Refugee Agency, help displaced people settle into your local community, or volunteer with a relief organization.

Having purchased this book and invested some of your time into reading about women in history, you have already done so much! You have been curious enough to rise above the pressures of daily life and think critically about our strange and wonderful past. You have understood that women's voices, be they refugees or rescuers, still need to be amplified today and that you can play a significant part in that effort.

If you would like to learn more about how these women and men saved thousands of people from horrible fates during WWII, then visit YouTube and search for the series *Rescuers: Stories of Courage*. The three distinct films, each holding two separate stories of rescuers across Europe throughout WWII, give a flavor of the time and illustrate the dangers faced by the women rescuers.

Finally, I would like to thank you for buying this book and for having an interest to learn about these women's lives. In a way, you are rescuing these heroes from obscurity and oblivion.

Please drop a comment and rating online so that I can hear your experience as a reader. And be sure to look out for my other books in the *Brave Women Who Changed the Course of WWII* series for more fascinating true stories.

And remember, we can all be heroes, we just need to take the first step forward.

Author

Elise Baker has had a lifelong interest in women's history and WWII. Her immediate family, from the borderlands of the Czech Republic, became stateless refugees and dispersed all over the world after the Second World War. Their riveting stories and Elise's mixed European heritage inspired a deep interest in this historical period. Elise is especially passionate about excavating the past to unearth the stories of women whose remarkable feats and accomplishments have been buried and forgotten because of their gender.

She holds a Bachelor of Arts degree in Humanities with a specialty in English Literature and a Postgraduate Diploma in Information Management. Her professional career has been in libraries and archives, and subsequently in television, in an editorial capacity. Elise is also a keen reader of both literary fiction and biographies, and she appreciates the variety of genres that makes history come alive to readers in exciting, accessible, and relatable ways.

References

Alberge, D. (2017, November 5). *Spy mystery of British sisters who helped Jewish refugees flee the Nazis*. The Guardian. https://www.theguardian.com/world/2017/nov/05/ida-louise-cook-sisters-helped-jewish-refugees-flee-nazis-spy-mystery-film

Andrée de Jongh. (2020, April 29). In *Wikipedia*. https://en.wikipedia.org/wiki/Andr%C3%A9e_de_Jongh

Atwood, K. (2011, June 27). *Women heroes of WWII: Ebba Lund: The girl with the red cap*. Women Heroes of WWII. http://womenheroesofwwii.blogspot.com/2011/06/ebba-lund-girl-with-red-cap.html

Brade, L. E. (2017). *Networks of escape: Jewish flight from the Bohemian lands, 1938–1941* [Doctoral dissertation, Department of History, University of North Carolina at Chapel Hill]. https://cdr.lib.unc.edu/downloads/r494vm50r

Cecilia Razovsky. (2021, October 29). In *Wikipedia*. https://en.wikipedia.org/wiki/Cecilia_Razovsky

Center for Jewish History. (n.d.). *Papers of Cecilia Razovsky, P-290*. Collection of the American Jewish Historical Society. https://archives.cjh.org/repositories/3/resources/20038

Child labor. (2009, October 27). History.
https://www.history.com/topics/
industrial-revolution/child-labor

Comet line. (2022, May 28). In *Wikipedia.*
https://en.wikipedia.org/wiki/Comet_Line

Cook, I. (2008). *Safe passage: The remarkable true story of two
sisters who rescued Jews from the Nazis.* Harlequin.

Corbett, S. (2007, December 30). The escape artist.
The New York Times.
https://www.nytimes.com/2007/12/30/
magazine/30dejongh-t.html

Danty, M. (n.d.). *Cecilia Razovsky.* The One Thousand
Children; YIVO Institute for Jewish Research.
https://onethousandchildren.yivo.org/
Cecilia-Razovsky

Denmark: a nation takes action. In *Holocaust and human
behavior.* (2017). Facing History and Ourselves.
https://www.facinghistory.org/holocaust-and-
human-behavior/chapter-9/denmark-nation-
takes-action

Doreen Warriner. (2022, May 25). In *Wikipedia.*
https://en.wikipedia.org/wiki/
Doreen_Warriner

Dzięciołowska, K. (2018, May). *Irena Sendler's children.*
POLIN Museum of the History of Polish Jews.
https://sprawiedliwi.org.pl/en/
o-sprawiedliwych/irena-sendlerowa/
dzieci-ireny-sendlerowej

Ebba Lund. (2022, January 25). In *Wikipedia.*
    https://en.wikipedia.org/wiki/Ebba_Lund#
    cite_note-:0-2

Eder, M. K. (2021). *The Girls who stepped out of line: Untold
    stories of the women who changed the course of World
    War II.* Sourcebooks.

Facts about Irena. (2014, May 10). *Life in a Jar: The Irena
    Sendler Project.*
    https://irenasendler.org/facts-about-irena/

Friedman, S. S. (1973). *No haven for the oppressed: United
    States policy towards Jewish refugees, 1938–1945.*
    Wayne State University Press.
    https://digital.library.wayne.edu/item/
    wayne:WayneStateUniversityPress4340/
    file/PDF_FULL

Ganey, M. (n.d.). *Biographical sketch of Cecilia Razovsky.*
    Alexander Street.
    https://documents.alexanderstreet.com/d/
    1011000464

Grenville, A. (2011, April). Doreen Warriner, Trevor
    Chadwick and the 'Winton children.' *AJR
    Journal* (4).
    https://ajr.org.uk/wp-content/uploads/
    2018/02/2011_april.pdf

Hájková, A. (2018, December 12). *The woman behind the
    Kindertransport.* History Today.
    https://www.historytoday.com/archive/
    feature/woman-behind-kindertransport

Hájková, A. (2022). *Marking a forgotten heroine.*
    The Jewish Chronicle.

https://www.thejc.com/news/uk-news/marking-the-life-of-a-forgotten-heroine-1.445765

Hammel, A. (2018, November 22). *The 1938 Kindertransport saved 10,000 children but it's hard to describe it as purely a success.* The Conversation. https://theconversation.com/the-1938-kindertransport-saved-10-000-children-but-its-hard-to-describe-it-as-purely-a-success-107299

Handcock, K. (2022, February 15). Irena Sendler: The woman who saved the lives of 2,500 Jewish children during the Holocaust. *A Mighty Girl.* https://www.amightygirl.com/blog?p=23101

Imperial War Museums. (n.d.). *Daily life in the Warsaw Ghetto.* https://www.iwm.org.uk/history/daily-life-in-the-warsaw-ghetto

Irena Sendler. (2019, August 17). In *Wikipedia.* https://en.wikipedia.org/wiki/Irena_Sendler

Jackson, A. (2019, January 8). *Dutch resistance.* Prezi. https://prezi.com/p/u6mn6k72igyz/dutch-resistance/

Kirby, P. (2022, May 9). *Why has Russia invaded Ukraine and what does Putin want?* BBC News. https://www.bbc.com/news/world-europe-56720589

Klinger, J. (2021, March 7). *Drive to honor Holocaust rescuer Marie Schmolka.* San Diego Jewish World. https://www.sdjewishworld.com/2021/03/06/drive-to-honor-holocaust-rescuer-marie-schmolka/

Kroll, C. (2009, July 11). *Irena Sendler: Rescuer of the children of Warsaw*. Chabad; The Jewish Woman. https://www.chabad.org/theJewishWoman/ article_cdo/aid/939081/jewish/ Irena-Sendler.htm

The Leslie Flint Trust. (2019, March 17). *Ida Cook and Louise Cook – wartime heroines* [Video]. YouTube. https://www.youtube.com/watch?v= j5F-mC8Go9w

Lund, T. (2014, January 31). *Ebba Lund*. Københavns Universitet. https://kub.ku.dk/biblioteker/frederiksberg/ landbohoejskolens-historie/life150/forskere/ ebba-lund/

Marie Schmolka. (2021, December 12). In *Wikipedia*. https://en.wikipedia.org/wiki/Marie_Schmolka

Martin, D. (2007, October 18). Andrée de Jongh, 90, legend of Belgian resistance, dies. *The New York Times*. https://www.nytimes.com/2007/10/18/ world/europe/18jongh.html

Mary Burchell. (2022, April 24). In *Wikipedia*. https://en.wikipedia.org/wiki/Mary_Burchell

Masters, J. (2020, February 5). *Ukraine: Conflict at the crossroads of Europe and Russia*. Council on Foreign Relations. https://www.cfr.org/backgrounder/ukraine-conflict-crossroads-europe-and-russia

Mayer, J. (2020). Irena Sendler and the girls from Kansas. *Humanities*, Summer 2020, Volume 41,

Number 3. The National Endowment for the Humanities. https://www.neh.gov/article/irena-sendler-and-girls-kansas

McCune, M. (1999, December 31). *Cecilia Razovsky.* Shalvi/Hyman Encyclopedia of Jewish Women; Jewish Women's Archive. https://jwa.org/encyclopedia/article/razovsky-cecilia

McEnchroe, T. (2019, May 18). *The hidden story of Doreen Warriner – academic turned humanitarian hero.* Radio Prague International; Czech Radio. https://english.radio.cz/hidden-story-doreen-warriner-academic-turned-humanitarian-hero-8130919

McFadden, R. D. (2015, July 1). Nicholas Winton, rescuer of 669 children from Holocaust, dies at 106. *The New York Times.* https://www.nytimes.com/2015/07/02/world/europe/nicholas-winton-is-dead-at-106-saved-children-from-the-holocaust.html

Miller, Y. A. (2017, November 19). *Ida and Louise Cook's remarkable rescue mission.* Aish. https://aish.com/ida-and-louise-cooks-remarkable-rescue-mission/

MoviesTime. (2022, January 30). *Rescuers: Stories of courage: Two women (1997)* [Video]. YouTube. https://www.youtube.com/watch?v=Zd0fnd9sJoc

The opera-loving sisters who "stumbled" into heroism. (2017, January 28). BBC News. https://www.bbc.com/news/uk-england-tyne-38732779

Neave, A. (2013). *Little Cyclone: The Girl Who Started The Comet Line.* Biteback Publishing Ltd. Originally edition 1954.

Peace for our time. (2022, June 5). In *Wikipedia.* https://en.wikipedia.org/wiki/Peace_for_our_time

Polskie Radio. (2016). *A new documentary about the life of Irena Sendler* [Video]. YouTube. https://www.youtube.com/watch?v=mpP2fvwPhkc

Quotes: Danish rescue and relief. (n.d.). Institute for the Study of Rescue and Altruism in the Holocaust. https://www.holocaustrescue.org/danish-rescue-quotes

Shipman, J. D. (2020). *Irena's War.* Kensington.

Shuff, D. (2010). *Evader: The epic story of the first British airman to be rescued by the Comete Escape Line in World War II.* The History Press.

Simkin, J. (1997, September). *Andree de Jongh.* Spartacus Educational. https://spartacus-educational.com/FRjongh.htm

Smith, M. K. (2017). *The Postwoman: Based on the true story of Andrée De Jongh.* Createspace Independent Publishing Platform.

Šmok, M. & Hájková, A. (2018, November 19). *About Marie Schmolka*. Marie Schmolka. https://marieschmolka.org/about-marie-schmolka/

Sunderland's "~Schindler sisters" honoured with blue plaque for heroism saving Jews from Nazis. (2016, December 9). Sunderland Echo. https://www.sunderlandecho.com/news/sunderlands-schindler-sisters-honoured-blue-plaque-heroism-saving-jews-nazis-362343

Tait, R. (2019, November 9). *Prague to honour little-known saviour of refugees fleeing Nazis*. The Guardian. https://www.theguardian.com/world/2019/nov/10/prague-honour-little-known-saviour-refugees-fleeing-nazis-marie-schmolka

Talbot, M. (2019, September 3). Ida and Louise Cook, two unusual heroines of the Second World War. *The New Yorker*. https://www.newyorker.com/books/second-read/ida-and-louise-cook-two-unusual-heroines-of-the-second-world-war

TED-Ed. (2021, June 28). *How one person saved over 2,000 children from the Nazis – Iseult Gillespie* [Video]. YouTube. https://www.youtube.com/watch?v=LxZkdQfgot8

The United States Holocaust Memorial Museum (USHMM). (2019a). *The Evian Conference*. Holocaust Encyclopedia. https://encyclopedia.ushmm.org/content/en/article/the-evian-conference

The United States Holocaust Memorial Museum
(USHMM). (n.d.). *King Christian X of Denmark.*
Holocaust Encyclopedia.
https://encyclopedia.ushmm.org/content/en/a
rticle/king-christian-x-of-denmark

The United States Holocaust Memorial Museum
(USHMM). (2009). *Nazi camps.* Holocaust
Encyclopedia.
https://encyclopedia.ushmm.org/content/
en/article/nazi-camps

The United States Holocaust Memorial Museum
(USHMM). (1994, June 10). *Oral history interview
with Ebba Lund.*
https://collections.ushmm.org/search/catalog/
irn513389

The United States Holocaust Memorial Museum
(USHMM). (2019b). *The United States and the
refugee crisis, 1938-41.* Holocaust Encyclopedia.
https://encyclopedia.ushmm.org/content/en/
article/the-united-states-and-the-refugee-crisis-
1938-41

The United States Holocaust Memorial Museum
(USHMM). (2014). *Warsaw Ghetto uprising.*
Holocaust Encyclopedia.
https://encyclopedia.ushmm.org/content/en/
article/warsaw-ghetto-uprising

Nicky van der Drift, N. (2020, May 26). *Andrée de Jongh.*
International Bomber Command Centre.
https://internationalbcc.co.uk/about-
ibcc/news/andree-de-jongh/#:~:text=

%E2%80%9CMy%20name%20is%20
Andr%C3%A9e%20%E2%80%A6%20but

Wallenstein, V. (2017, October 18). *The Jewish refugee crisis in WWII* [Video]. YouTube. https://www.youtube.com/watch?v= UsxMSrbSNLM

Warriner, D. (1984). Winter in Prague. *The Slavonic and East European Review, 62(2)*, 209–240. https://www.jstor.org/stable/4208852?socuuid =055c8758-8806-48e7-b71c-88ab9d423a99

Werner, E. E. (2004). *A conspiracy of decency: The rescue of the Danish Jews during World War II.* Westview Press.

Willoughby, I. (2019, November 11). *Saviour of Jewish refugees Marie Schmolka finally honoured in Prague.* Radio Prague International. https://english.radio.cz/saviour-jewish-refugees-marie-schmolka-finally-honoured-prague-8115797

Winters, M. (2019, October 22). *Ebba Lund.* Prezi. https://prezi.com/p/52y6dp7xoqvs/ebba-lund/

Wolfisz, F. (2016, April 1). *The quiet courage of sisters who saved 29 Jewish families.* Jewish News. https://www.jewishnews.co.uk/the-quiet-courage-of-sisters-who-saved-29-jewish-families/

Wondrium. (2020, October 19). *The unsung heroes of World War 2: Andree de Jongh and the resistance* [Video]. YouTube.

https://www.youtube.com/watch?v= RhcjylrhRas

World Jewish Congress. (2018). *Irena Sendler: The Polish woman who saved 2,500 Jewish children* [Video]. YouTube. https://www.youtube.com/watch?v= vg4deegQxH4

Zucker, B.-A. (2008). *Cecilia Razovsky and the American Jewish women's rescue operations in the Second World War*. Vallentine Mitchell.

Zucker, B.-A. (2021). Cecilia Razovsky, the American activist who rescued German Jewish children (1933–1945). *Women in Judaism: A Multidisciplinary E-Journal*, 17(2). https://doi.org/10.33137/wij.v17i2.36882

Image References

Figure 1. WikiImages. (2013, January 4). *Ghetto Warsaw fear child armed up* [Image]. Pixabay. https://pixabay.com/photos/ghetto-warsaw-fear-child-armed-67736/

Figure 2. Fazacas, B. (2021, March 22). *Fabryka 'Emalia' Oskara Schindlera* [Image]. Unsplash. https://unsplash.com/photos/RhvXVO16zqw

Figure 3. Burke, T. (2019, March 2). *Dachau main entrance gate* [Image]. Unsplash. https://unsplash.com/photos/4Kr-HCx-Y6c

Figure 4. Estate of Ida Cook and Rupert Crew Limited. (1926). *Ida & Louise Cook on the eve of their trip to New York, 1926* [Image]. Victoria and Albert Museum, London.

Figure 5. AJHS. (2022, July 25). *Cecilia Razovsky amongst friends* [Image]. Photo courtesy of the American Jewish Historical Society, from the Papers of Cecilia Razovsky (P-290), Box 7, Folder 20. https://digipres.cjh.org/delivery/DeliveryManagerServlet?dps_pid=IE845162

Figure 6. Wikimedia Commons. (1942). Irena Sendler: Unknown author (https://commons.wikimedia.org/wiki/File:Irena_Sendlerowa_1942.jpg), *"Irena Sendlerowa 1942"*, marked as public domain, more details on Wikimedia Commons: https://commons.wikimedia.org/wiki/Template:PD-1996

Figure 7. *Identification card for Ebba Lund from the Polytechnic Institute* [Image]. (n.d.). Frihedsmuseet 07B-13908-4, The Museum of Danish Resistance 1940-1945.

Figure 8. S. Spak. (n.d.). Sidor Spak (1885–1950) (https://commons.wikimedia.org/wiki/File:Marie_Schmolkova_1893_1940.jpg), *"Marie Schmolkova 1893 1940"*, marked as public domain, more details on Wikimedia Commons: https://commons.wikimedia.org/wiki/Template:PD-old {{PD-1996}} – public domain in its source country on January 1, 1996 and in the United States.

Figure 9. *Mrs. Doreen Warriner* Author of this photo is unknown person. (https://commons.wikimedia.org/wiki/File:Mrs.Doreen.Warriner.(1904-1972).BW.gif), *"Mrs.Doreen.Warriner.(1904-1972).BW"*, marked as public domain, more details on Wikimedia Commons: https://commons.wikimedia.org/wiki/Template:PD-anon-70

Figure 10. *Twenty-five year old Andrée de Jongh* [Image]. (1946, February). Imperial War Museum (HU 55451). https://www.iwm.org.uk/collections/item/object/205028563

Figure 11. Clinch, J. (2007, April). *Jim Cromar (Mad Cromar) Comet Line number one escaper* [Image]. www.belgiumww2.info.
http://home.clara.net/clinchy/neeball.htm

Figure 12. Brown, R. (2018, January 4). *Fight like a girl* [Image]. Unsplash.
https://unsplash.com/photos/OedMkCaf_7o

Acknowledgments

Image of the Cook sisters — Photograph reproduced by kind permission of the Estate of Ida Cook and Rupert Crew Limited © Victoria and Albert Museum, London.

Image of Cecilia Razovsky — Great thanks go to The American Jewish Historical Society for their permission to use the image of Razovsky through her published *Papers of Cecilia Razovsky*.

Images of Irena Sendler, Marie Schmolka, and Doreen Warriner — Courtesy of Wikimedia Commons Images.

Image of Ebba Lund – Many thanks to The Museum of Danish Resistance for sourcing and granting permission to use this image.

Image of Andrée de Jongh — Courtesy of the Imperial War Museum © IWM HU 55451 under Civilian Bravery Awards During the Second World War.

Image of Jim Cromar — Thank you to the www.belgiumww2.info Escape Line Research and Remembrance website and John Clinch for the permission to use his image.

Other Books by Elise Baker

Women Code Breakers: The Best Kept Secret of WWII
True Stories of Female Code Breakers Whose Top-Secret Work Helped Win WWII

Nightingales, Bluebirds and Angels of Mercy
True Stories of the Courage and Heroism of Nurses on the Frontlines in WWII

Princess, Countess, Socialite, Spy
True Stories of High-Society Ladies Turned WWII Spies

Printed in Great Britain
by Amazon

25190597R00108